STAR WARS™

ENCYCLOPEDIA OF
STARFIGHTERS
AND OTHER VEHICLES

WRITTEN BY
LANDRY Q. WALKER

CONTENTS

The vehicles in this book are split into chapters based on where they usually operate: on land, in the air, in water, or in space. You can look up the page number for a vehicle below, or use the index at the back of the book.

Introduction 4

AIR 6
Zam's Airspeeder 8
Jedi Turbo Speeder 9
ComortRide Passenger Airspeeder 10
Speeder Bus 11
Coruscant Fire Suppression Ship 12
Coruscant Police Speeder 13
T-16 Skyhopper 14
STAP 15
HMP Droid Gunship 16
LAAT 17
Pteropter 18
Wookiee Catamaran 19
Snowspeeder 20
Cloud Car 21
TIE Striker 22
TIE Reaper 23

LAND 24
Anakin's Podracer 26
Sebulba's Podracer 27
Maul's Speeder Bike 28
Flitknot Speeder 29

Barc Speeder 30
Freeco Bike 31
Undicur-class Jumpspeeder 32
Mandalorian Speeder 33
Starhawk Speeder 34
Nightsister Speeder 35
74-Z Speeder Bike 36
Joben T-85 Speeder 37
Rey's Speeder 38
Landspeeders 39
Gian Speeder 40
Clone Swamp Speeder 41
Mandalorian Police Speeder 42
Luke's Landspeeder 43
Canto Bight Police Speeder 44
Ski Speeder 45
MTT 46
AAT Battle Tank 47
Defoliator Tank 48
Super Tank 49
Stun Tank 50
Pirate Tank 51
Umbaran Hover Tank 52
Imperial Troop Transport 53
Khetanna 54
Desert Skiff 55
Spider Droid 56
Dwarf Spider Droid 57
SPHA-T 58
AT-TE 59
AT-OT 60
AT-RT 61
AT-DP 62
AT-ST 63

AT-AT 64
AT-ACT 65
AT-M6 66
Gungan Battle Wagon 67
Hailfire Droid 68
Corporate Alliance Tank Droid 69
Wheel Bike 70
Clone Turbo Tank 71
Imperial Assault Tank 72
Sandcrawler 73

WATER 74
Gondola Speeder 76
Naboo Water Speeder 77
Hutt Swamp Speeder 78
Tribubble Bongo 79
Kamino Submarine 80
OMS Devilfish Sub 81
Quarren UTS Pike 82
Trident-class Assault Ship 83

SPACE 84
Escape Pods 86
Droch-class Boarding Ship 87
Tactical Infiltration Pod 88
Naboo Starfighter 89
Vulture Droid 90
Hyena Bomber 91
Geonosian Starfighter 92

Fanblade Fighter	93	
Soulless One	94	
Tri-Fighter	95	
Delta-7 Light Interceptor	96	
ETA-2 Light Interceptor	97	
V-19 Torrent Starfighter	98	
V-wing	99	
ARC-170 Starfighter	100	
Umbaran Starfighter	101	
Gauntlet Starfighter	102	
Fang Fighter	103	
Xanadu Blood	104	
TIE Fighter	105	
TIE Bomber	106	
TIE Interceptor	107	
TIE Advanced V1	108	
TIE Advanced X1	109	
TIE Defender	110	
Mining Guild TIE Fighter	111	
A-wing	112	
Blade Wing	113	
B-wing	114	
U-wing	115	
T-65 X-wing	116	
Y-wing	117	
Special Forces TIE Fighter	118	
TIE Silencer	119	
T-70 X-wing	120	
Resistance Bomber	121	
H-Type Nubian Yacht	122	
Naboo Star Skiff	123	
Scimitar	124	
Sheathipede Shuttle	125	
Sheathipede-class Type B	126	
Solar Sailer	127	
Maxillipede Shuttle	128	
Republic Attack Shuttle	129	
T-6 Shuttle	130	
ETA-class Shuttle	131	
H-2 Executive Shuttle	132	
GX1 Short Hauler	133	

Theta-class T-2C Shuttle	134	
Mandalorian Shuttle	135	
Flarestar-class Attack Shuttle	136	
Taylander Shuttle	137	
Phantom	138	
Phantom II	139	
Star Commuter 2000	140	
Delta-class T-3C Shuttle	141	
Lambda-class Shuttle	142	
Sentinel-class Shuttle	143	
Zeta-class Cargo Shuttle	144	
Upsilon-class Shuttle	145	
Slave I	146	
Twilight	147	
Halo	148	
Hound's Tooth	149	
Turtle Tanker	150	
Moogan Gunship	151	
Pantoran Cruiser	152	
Ghost	153	
Lancer-class Pursuit Craft	154	
YT-2400 Light Freighter	155	
Millennium Falcon	156	
Dornean Gunship	157	
Republic Tugboat	158	
Quadjumper	159	
AA-9 Coruscant Freighter	160	
Zygerrian Slave Ship	161	
Vulture's Claw	162	
Imperial Freighter	163	
IGV-55 Surveillance Vessel	164	
Imperial Cargo Ship	165	
Broken Horn	166	
Eravana	167	
Naboo Royal Starship	168	
Naboo Royal Cruiser	169	
CSS-1 Corellian Star Shuttle	170	
Crucible	171	
Luxury Yacht	172	
TIE Silencer	173	

Trade Federation Landing Ship	174	
Techno Union Starship	175	
Separatist Supply Ship	176	
Acclamator-class Assault Ship	177	
Rebel Transport	178	
First Order Transporter	179	
Resistance Transport	180	
Separatist Frigate	181	
Republic Frigate	182	
Pelta-class Frigate	183	
Stealth Ship	184	
Acushnet	185	
Imperial Interdictor	186	
Imperial Light Carrier	187	
Tantive IV	188	
Hammerhead Corvette	189	
Rebel Cruiser	190	
Trade Federation Battleship	191	
Malevolence	192	
Invisible Hand	193	
Republic Attack Cruiser	194	
Coronet	195	
Imperial Star Destroyer	196	
Executor	197	
Profundity	198	
Home One	199	
Raddus	200	
Finalizer	201	
Supremacy	202	
Imperial Construction Module	203	
Death Star	204	
Death Star II	205	
Index	206	
Acknowledgments	208	

FROM MIGHTY BATTLESTATIONS to the fastest hunk of junk around, the galaxy is filled with vehicles of every shape and size. There are speeders for traveling in style, starfighters for completing critical missions, freighters for smuggling cargo, and many other types of vehicle besides. Galactic governments, rebel groups, and illegal gangs could not exist without vehicles to travel between, above, and across worlds.

AIR

ZAM'S AIRSPEEDER

KORO-2 AIRSPEEDER

TYPE: Airspeeder
MANUFACTURER: Desler
Gizh Outworld Mobility
Corporation
SPEED: 1,200 kph (745 mph)
MODEL: Koro-2 all-
environment exodrive
airspeeder
LENGTH: 6.6 m (21 ft 7 in)
WEAPONS: None

THE KORO-2 IS A small personal airspeeder. It is
fairly unusual, as it can also travel under water or in
space to a limited degree. This makes the Koro-2
a popular choice of getaway vehicle with criminals.

Caught in the Act

Bounty hunter Zam Wesell uses one of these vehicles
during her attempt to assassinate Senator Amidala.

Pressurized
2-person cockpit

Electromagnetic
propulsion system in
forward mandibles

After Zam's assassination attempt fails,
Obi-Wan Kenobi and Anakin Skywalker
chase her across the planet Coruscant.

POWERED UP

The Koro-2 speeders use an
electromagnetic field for
propulsion. The cabin holds an air
supply that will last for two weeks.

JEDI TURBO SPEEDER

PRAXIS MK. 1 TURBO SPEEDER

AN ELEGANTLY DESIGNED TURBO speeder, the Praxis Mk. 1 is piloted by members of the Jedi Order when traveling around the city planet of Coruscant. Its thin, wedge-like design cuts down on wind resistance, and the navigation systems are programed to bypass heavy traffic.

Red denotes official government business in the Republic

Jedi Master Plo Koon

Captain Rex and Anakin Skywalker take a turbo speeder to help Ahsoka Tano when she is falsely accused of murder.

Symbol of the Jedi Order

SAFETY FIRST

The Praxis Mk. 1 turbo speeder is equipped with collision-detection systems to help its pilot avoid accidents. Twin repulsor generators allow the ship to turn upside-down in midair.

Jedi Colors

Anakin Skywalker and Ahsoka Tano's brightly colored turbo speeder contrasts with the murky underworld of Coruscant as the pair investigate an attack on the Jedi Temple.

COMFORTRIDE PASSENGER AIRSPEEDER

CORUSCANT AIR TAXI

DATA FILE

TYPE: Repulsorcraft
MANUFACTURER: Hyrotii Corporation
SPEED: 191 kph (119 mph)
MODEL: ComfortRide
LENGTH: 10.5 m (34 ft 5 in)
WEAPONS: None

THE REPULSOR-POWERED

ComfortRide airspeeder is a popular means of traveling around large cities. Unlike personal vehicles, this passenger transport is allowed to fly outside official skylanes.

The Hyrotii Corporation also manufacture the cheaper and less luxurious EasyRide airspeeder.

Air traffic control signal receivers inside hull

Seating for 4 or more passengers

3 multi-spectrum headlights

Housing for radial repulsor steering array

SAFE TRAVELS

When it comes to the design of the airspeeder, comfort and security are priorities. A tractor field holds passengers safely in place. There is a forward-facing fin to keep the vehicle stable, while repulsor engines ensure a smooth ride for everyone aboard.

ComfortRide Crash

Duchess Satine's Kryze's ComfortRide is tampered with by a group called the Death Watch. The Duchess and her guards manage to jump to safety— just before the speeder crashes!

SPEEDER BUS

AIR TRANSPORT

DATA FILE

TYPE: Speeder bus
MANUFACTURER: GoCorp
SPEED: 300 kph (186 mph)
MODEL: Util-313
LENGTH: 18 m (59 ft)
WEAPONS: None

THESE SPECIALIZED SHUTTLES ARE used by members of the Galactic Senate, high-ranking Republic military personnel, and the Jedi Order. They are designed for travel within cities and provide passengers with a luxurious experience.

Pilot's cockpit

Transparent roof

Repulsor engine

OFFICIAL ESCORT
Shuttle buses are sometimes used to carry high-ranking officials. On these occasions, fighter escorts are deployed by the Senate to accompany the airbus, providing its passengers with safe passage to their destination.

The shuttle bus is made using a see-through material called transparisteel. This gives passengers a 360-degree view.

Hero's Welcome
After the Battle of Coruscant, Supreme Chancellor Palpatine, Obi-Wan Kenobi, and Anakin Skywalker travel to the Senate Building on a Jedi shuttle bus.

CORUSCANT FIRE SUPPRESSION SHIP

EMERGENCY FIRESPEEDER

DATA FILE

TYPE: Speeder
MANUFACTURER:
Rothana Heavy Engineering
SPEED: 1,100 kph
(683 mph)
MODEL: F-143
LENGTH: 36 m (118 ft 1 in)
WEAPONS: Water spray,
foam spray, fire retardant
agents

THE FIRE SUPPRESSION SHIPS are a welcome sight in the skies above the bustling city-planet of Coruscant. They are crewed by members of the Coruscant Rescue Ops. This organization exists only to serve the greater good of the city by providing essential disaster relief whenever necessary.

The brave members of the Coruscant Rescue Ops are equipped with radiation-proof suits and handheld fire suppression hoses.

DISASTER-READY

A fireship's undercarriage includes a number of tanks full of water and foam. It is also equipped with a medical bay, allowing crewmembers to treat serious injuries quickly.

Pressurized dousers spray water or foam

Emergency lights

Put out the Flame

During the Battle of Coruscant, a ship named the *Invisible Hand* crashes down to the planet's surface. Fireships spray it with water to put out the flames.

Heat-resistant cockpit

Water tanks

Tractor beam projector removes debris

CORUSCANT POLICE SPEEDER

LAW ENFORCEMENT AIRSPEEDER

DATA FILE

TYPE: Speeder
MANUFACTURER: SoroSuub
Corporation
SPEED: 350 kph (217 mph)
MODEL: Panther police
interceptor
LENGTH: 5.1 m (16 ft 8 in)
WEAPONS: None

POLICE SPEEDERS ARE A vital part of the security systems of Coruscant, and are a common sight in the airways of the great Galactic City. Unlike most civilian craft, police speeders are not bound to airlanes and can maneuver freely, so that they can respond to crimes quickly.

Police speeders are piloted by 501-Z police droids, provided by the SoroSuub Corporation. The droids are programmed to calm dangerous situations.

Sirens and emergency lights

Bars for prisoner transport

Turbine engine

Spotlight

LAW SPEEDER

Each police speeder is outfitted with a bright spotlight on one side, and features flashing red and blue lights for emergencies. The rear compartment serves as a temporary prison cell.

On the Lookout

While escaping from a pair of murderous bounty hunters, Senator Padmé Amidala attracts the attention of several Coruscant police speeders.

T-16 SKYHOPPER

PERSONAL REPULSORLIFT AIRSPEEDER

DATA FILE

TYPE: Airspeeder
MANUFACTURER: Incom
Corporation
SPEED: 1,200 kph
(745 mph)
MODEL: T-16
HEIGHT 10.4 m (34 ft 1 in)
WEAPONS: Customizable

BECAUSE OF ITS SPEED and its ability to reach high atmospheres, the T-16 Skyhopper is a popular craft choice across the galaxy. While these airspeeders are favored by civilians, their limited weapons capacity means they are largely ignored by the Imperial Military.

After the fall of the Empire, civilians celebrate in the streets. A T-16 flies over the crowded streets of Mos Eisley.

Stabilizing fin wing
in tri-wing design

Pressurized cockpit

ADD-ONS

The T-16's third wing gives it increased stability. The ship has optional weapons upgrades, including stun cannons, pneumatic cannons, and laser cannons.

Ion engine

Pneumatic projectile gun
for blasting womp rats

Toy Ship

Owen Lars gives a T-16 to his nephew, Luke Skywalker. Luke also builds a small model version of the ship to play with when he doesn't feel like actually flying.

STAP

SINGLE TROOPER AERIAL PLATFORM

DATA FILE

TYPE: Repulsorlift craft
MANUFACTURER: Baktoid Armor Workshop
SPEED: 400 kph (248 mph)
MODEL: Single Trooper Aerial Platform
HEIGHT: 2.9 m (9 ft 6 in)
WEAPONS: 2 blaster cannons

THE STAP IS A POPULAR CRAFT used on many worlds for both military and civilian transport. Its simplicity allows for reliable, but inexpensive, construction. However, during combat, the STAP's lack of shielding leads to a high casualty rate among pilots—mainly expendable droid units.

Blaster cannon

Energy-cell powered drive turbines

DROID VEHICLE

STAPs are the vehicle of choice for droid armies. The craft's onboard computer syncs with the droid control station for more coordinated, efficient maneuvers.

Stability footlocks

A prison warden and enemy of the Republic, Osi Sobeck attempts to lead a droid force into battle aboard a STAP.

Naboo Invasion

The Trade Federation adopts STAPs as part of its military. The organization relies heavily on these vehicles in its ill-fated invasion of Naboo.

HMP DROID GUNSHIP

HEAVY MISSILE PLATFORM

DATA FILE

TYPE: Gunship
MANUFACTURER: Baktoid
Fleet Ordnance
SPEED: 600 kph (373 mph)
MODEL: Heavy Missile
Platform droid gunship
LENGTH: 12.4 m (40 ft 8 in)
WEAPONS: Multi-missile
racks, wingtip laser
cannons, 2 laser cannon
turrets, antipersonnel
laser cannon

ALSO KNOWN AS the HMP Predator, this gunship is a vessel in only the strictest sense. It requires no pilot and instead uses an advanced droid brain to think for itself—while always remaining loyal to the Separatists.

Air Pressure
HMPs play a large part in the Separatists' oppression of the planet Onderon. One squadron almost wipes out the entire planet's resistance force.

Reactor core

Missile-guidance rangefinder

Photoreceptor "eye"

Mission-specific missiles

NEAR OR FAR
HMPs are adaptable for a range of mission profiles. Different laser cannons are fitted on the basis of whether an assault will be long range or at close quarters.

Rotating laser cannon turret

The HMP gunships are part of the vast Separatist forces during the Battle of Kashyyyk.

LAAT

LOW ALTITUDE ASSAULT TRANSPORT

THE DEPENDABLE LAAT IS one of the Republic's main deployment craft. Heavily armored and highly maneuverable, this war transport is often sent into combat under fire. It can glide through a storm of lasers to safely land its cargo and troops.

Boost chamber

BRANCH OUT

The LAAT is originally designed for low-atmosphere flights, giving it a distinct advantage over most high-altitude fighters in near-ground combat. However, later models are able to make short trips through deep space.

Gunner

Swivel laser cannon

Making a Mark

The standard LAATi can carry 30 clone troopers into battle. These clone trooper squads often decorate the sides of their LAATi with art.

The LAATc is rigged with docking clamps to haul AT-TEs into battle.

PTEROPTER

MSP80 HOVER POD

DATA FILE

TYPE: Speeder
MANUFACTURER: Gallofree
Aerial Products
SPEED: 30 kph (18 mph)
MODEL: MSP80
LENGTH: 4.1 m (13 ft 5 in)
WEAPONS: Rotary repeating
blaster cannon, 2 laser
cannons

THE PTEROPTER HOVER POD is bulky and unresponsive compared to most other speeders. However, its ability to switch between vertical and horizontal thrust is unmatched by any other vehicle of its class. The rotating blaster can pivot in any direction, independent of the speeder.

ON THE HUNT

Pteropters are traditionally used in mining operations, but these floating speeders become popular amongst Trandoshan hunters.

Tally of successful captures

Protective mesh

A Trandoshan named Garnac flies a customized Pteropter during his hunts. It is painted to look like a ferocious beast.

Headlights help keep prey in view

Tow hook and line for tethering small craft

Rotary repeating blaster cannon

Big Game

When Ahsoka Tano is imprisoned on the moon Wasskah, she finds herself hunted by several Trandoshans. They use these unique speeders to navigate the jungle terrain.

WOOKIEE CATAMARAN

OEVVAOR JET CATAMARAN

OEVVAOR CATAMARANS ARE NAMED after a ferocious sea creature from the planet Kashyyyk. They are used by civilians on the Wookiee homeworld, and are repurposed into military machines when the Clone Wars begin. These speeders can travel in both air and water.

DATA FILE

TYPE: Speeder
MANUFACTURER: Appazanna Engineering Works
SPEED: 370 kph (596 mph)
MODEL: Oevvaor
LENGTH: 15.1 m (49 ft 6 in)
WEAPONS: Blaster cannon, missile launcher (optional)

Dual rudders

Oevvaor catamarans are put into use during the Battle of Kashyyyk.

Two seats per hull

Pushrod links rudder to steering controls

Podracer-style engines

IN FLIGHT

The Oevvaor catamarans' twin repulsor generators provide thrust, while a small rotor aids upward flight. Armored windshields offer passengers limited protection.

Hull made from the wood of wroshyr trees

Armed for War

The Oevvaors are not originally outfitted with any weapons. However, after the Separatist Alliance invades Kashyyyk, missile launchers and repeating blasters are added to the design.

SNOWSPEEDER

REBEL AIRSPEEDER

DATA FILE

TYPE: Reconnaissance craft
MANUFACTURER: Incom Corporation
SPEED: 1,100 kph (683 mph)
MODEL: Modified T-47 Airspeeder
LENGTH: 5.3 m (17 ft 5 in)
WEAPONS: Harpoon gun and tow cable, 2 laser cannons

MEET THE ENEMY OF the Imperial walker. This seemingly simple airspeeder, modified for cold temperatures, is not well armed or shielded. However, its handy tow cables, added for non-combat purposes, earn this humble airship an honored place in the history books after the Battle of Hoth.

Harpoon gun

BASE SEARCHES

The rebels use the swift and maneuverable snowspeeders for searches, usually to scout around planetary bases.

Laser cannon

Rebel Defense

These low-altitude ships were never built for combat purposes. When the Empire strikes with full force in the Battle of Hoth, the rebels fight back with whatever is at their disposal.

In a decisive maneuver, Wedge Antilles ties his snowspeeder's cable around an AT-AT's legs, tangling them up and making the walker fall to the ground.

CLOUD CAR

DATA FILE

TYPE: Atmospheric repulsorcraft
MANUFACTURER: Bespin Motors
SPEED: 1,500 kph (932 mph)
MODEL: Storm IV Twin-Pod
LENGTH: 7 m (22 ft 11 in)
WEAPONS: 2 light blaster cannons

THE SKIES OVER Bespin are constantly dotted with this unusual vehicle. Developed locally within the system by Bespin Motors, the distinctive, twin-pod cloud car achieves a low orbit by using its repulsorlift system.

Keepers of Peace

The cloud cars are used as peacekeeping vehicles. They soar through the atmosphere of the gas giant Bespin, patrolling the airways and monitoring incoming traffic to the planet's mining colonies.

Pilot's pod with armored canopy

Gunner in gunner's pod

Armor-plated shell

Repulsorlift engine

Blaster cannon

DOUBLE ROLE

The ship is crewed by a pilot and a gunner. Each pod has all the equipment necessary to serve either role—a useful strategy in case one pod is ever damaged.

When Han Solo flies the *Millennium Falcon* into Cloud City, cloud cars escort the ship to the landing pad.

TIE STRIKER

TIE/SK ATMOSPHERIC FIGHTER

THE TIE STRIKER HAS a more aerodynamic design than the standard TIE fighter, as it is specifically created to operate within a planet's atmosphere. This makes it ideal for running patrol missions over planetary installations. Strikers are a common sight in the skies of worlds controlled by Imperials.

When rebels attack the Imperial installation at Scarif, TIE strikers are scrambled to serve as defense.

Solar energy collector panels

Mount can change angle of wings

Larger central pod than conventional TIE fighters

Heavy laser cannon

EXTRA SPACE

The TIE striker features a more spacious cockpit than the TIE fighter. There is enough room for an optional gunner station to be installed. Its wings can angle downward to add extra protection to the cockpit.

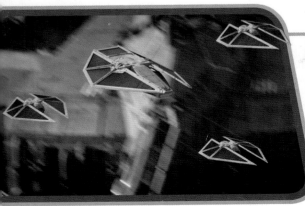

Protection

In addition to acting as patrol and defense ships, TIE strikers are often used as escort vehicles. They protect more vulnerable troop transports, such as the TIE reaper.

TIE REAPER

TWIN ION ENGINE REAPER

DATA FILE

TYPE: Dropship
MANUFACTURER: Sienar Fleet Systems
SPEED: 950 kph (590 mph)
MODEL: Twin Ion Engine reaper
LENGTH: 33.9 m (111 ft 2 in)
HYPERDRIVE: None
WEAPONS: 2 laser cannons

STREAMLINED FOR maximum speed within a planetary atmosphere, the TIE reaper is designed for deploying troops in the heat of battle. It is not primarily a combat vessel, and is less heavily armed than other TIE variants, so sometimes travels with a powerful escort of TIE strikers.

Diving Board
A ramp at the front of the TIE reaper allows it to drop its troops without landing—as seen over water in the Battle of Scarif.

Access hatch

Magnatonic locking mechanism

Solar collector

Deployment ramp

Reapers are sometimes used to deploy the elite Imperial soldiers known as death troopers.

ARTIC CONDITIONS
Much like the TIE striker, the reaper has articulated wings to assist with rapid vertical takeoff and landing.

LAND

ANAKIN'S PODRACER

BOONTA EVE CLASSIC WINNER

DATA FILE

TYPE: Repulsorcraft
MANUFACTURER: Custom
SPEED: 947 kph (588 mph)
MODEL: Podracer
LENGTH: 7 m (22 ft 11 in)
WEAPONS: None

YOUNG ANAKIN Skywalker builds his own podracer out of discarded machine parts that nobody else wants. In his talented hands, these cast-off pieces gain a new life, and his podracer becomes one of the fastest and most maneuverable ever built. Only someone with Anakin's deep connection to the Force can pilot it.

JAWA JUNK

Anakin's podracer is utterly unique. One of its engines was built from junk, while the other was bought from Jawas. It uses a one-of-a-kind fuel-injection system that Anakin designed himself.

Cockpit seats one

Steelton control cable

Energy binder arc

Triple air scoops

Optimistic Racer

Despite never having finished a race, Anakin convinces the Jedi Qui-Gon Jinn that he can win the Boonta Eve Classic. He does so, and his winnings pay for vital repairs to Queen Amidala's ship.

Jar Jar Binks gets a shock when he gets too close to the electrical binders in Anakin's podracer!

SEBULBA'S PODRACER

CHAMPION SHIP

DATA FILE

TYPE: Repulsorcraft
MANUFACTURER: Custom
SPEED: 829 kph (515 mph)
MODEL: Podracer
LENGTH: 7.5 m (24 ft 7 in)
WEAPONS: Flamethrowers, magna-spikes, ion disrupters

SEBULBA'S BRIGHT ORANGE podracer is a famous sight on the racetracks of Tatooine. Sebulba has no problem with cheating, and has installed illegal modifications to help him win. He is considered almost unbeatable—until he faces Anakin Skywalker in the Boonta Eve Classic.

Cockpit

Energy binder arc

WINNING WAYS

Sebulba uses special fuel to give his podracer an added edge. The vehicle is also equipped with numerous weapons so Sebulba can neutralize his opponents.

Air intake

Sebulba's podracer blows apart when he tries to force his competition off the racetrack. The cheat escapes unharmed.

Stabilizing vane

Fast and Furious

When racing young Anakin Skywalker, Sebulba rams his challenger's smaller podracer repeatedly. Anakin is the only other entrant who stands a chance of beating him.

MAUL'S SPEEDER BIKE

SPEEDER FOR A SITH

DATA FILE

TYPE: Repulsorcraft
MANUFACTURER: Razalon
SPEED: 650 kph (403 mph)
MODEL: FC-20
speeder bike
LENGTH: 1.6 m
(5 ft 3 in)
WEAPONS:
None

THE SITH LORD DARTH MAUL pilots a modified FC-20 on the planet Tatooine. Capable of pin-sharp turns, this compact speeder bike is popular with assassins and other criminals, who would be easier to track on larger vehicles.

Repulsorlift engine compartment

SMALL PROBLEMS
Its small size makes the FC-20 stealthy, but leaves limited room for engines. Consequently, it needs frequent recharging.

Steering controls

Pilot's seat

Footholds

Darth Maul calls his modified FC-20 *Bloodfin*. He has stripped it of all weapons and sensors to make it lighter and faster.

Duel Control
When Darth Maul leaps from his FC-20 to duel Jedi Master Qui-Gon Jinn, the speeder bike comes to an immediate stop, sensing that its pilot is no longer aboard.

28

FLITKNOT SPEEDER

DOOKU'S SPEEDER

DATA FILE

TYPE: Repulsorcraft
MANUFACTURER:
Huppla Pasa Tisc
Shipwrights Collective
SPEED: 634 kph (394 mph)
MODEL: Flitknot speeder
LENGTH: 3.2 m (10 ft 6 in)
WEAPONS: None

THE STANDARD FLITKNOT speeder is designed for scouting missions and is not equipped with weapons. However, Geonosian drones may ride flitknot speeders into battle, firing their handheld sonic blasters.

Rear-view display

Altitude controls

Stabilizer fin

COUNT'S CRAFT

Dooku's flitknot speeder has been modified for non-Geonosians. While traveling on his speeder, he is often escorted by starfighters.

Foothold

Stolen Speeder

Anakin Skywalker steals Dooku's Flitknot and uses it to travel across the Dune Sea of Tatooine.

Sith Lord Count Dooku uses his modified Flitknot speeder to flee Republic forces in the first Battle of Geonosis.

BARC SPEEDER

BIKER ADVANCED RECON COMMANDO SPEEDER

DATA FILE

TYPE: Speeder
MANUFACTURER: Aratech
Repulsor Company
SPEED: 520 kph (323 mph)
MODEL: Biker Advanced
Recon Commando speeder
LENGTH: 4.6 m (15 ft 1 in)
WEAPONS: 2 light
blaster cannons

THIS POWERFUL SPEEDER BIKE is designed for use by ARC (Advanced Recon Commando) troopers, but goes on to be piloted by other Republic fighters during the Clone Wars. Ideal for scouting missions, it is also used by police patrols on Coruscant.

Anakin Skywalker

One of two thrusters

Airscoop

Stabilizer fin

Light blaster cannon

CHOOSING SIDES

BARC speeders can be customized with mission-specific sidecars. These include stretchers and gunner pods, which can reverse direction to fire backwards.

Clone troopers pilot BARC speeders alongside Jedi Stass Allie, seconds before Order 66 compels them to betray her.

Battle Bike

Anakin Skywalker and Ahsoka Tano ride a BARC speeder with a sidecar as they lead the 501st Battalion into combat. Their mission: to defend the Togruta colony of Kiros from Separatist battle droids.

FREECO BIKE

CK-6 SWOOP BIKE

DATA FILE

TYPE: Repulsorcraft
MANUFACTURER:
Bespin Motors
SPEED: 440 kph
(273 mph)
MODEL: CK-6 swoop
LENGTH: 5.8 m (19 ft)
WEAPONS: Twin
laser cannons

NICKNAMED "FREECO" BECAUSE IT is used in freezing cold conditions, the CK-6 swoop bike is designed for use by clone cold assault troopers. It has an enclosed, heated cockpit, but the rest of the bike remains at risk of freezing.

Heated cockpit

Thruster

Multi-spectrum headlights

Repulsor grapple

Landing ski

SNOW WAY IN
The thrusters on the CK-6 have electrostatic baffles to keep ice and snow out, and heaters intended to stop the engines freezing. These measures have only limited success, however.

Clone Captain Rex wears special cold-weather gear to go with his CK-6 on the icy world of Orto Plutonia.

Ice Explorers
Freeco bikes are mostly used for scouting and reconnaisance missions on icy worlds. They are armed with twin laser cannons, but are of little use in combat situations.

UNDICUR-CLASS JUMPSPEEDER

JEDI SPEEDER BIKE

DATA FILE

TYPE: Repulsorlift vehicle
MANUFACTURER: Kuat Vehicles
SPEED: 250 kph (155 mph)
MODEL: *Undicur*-class
LENGTH: 1.8 m (5 ft 11 in)
WEAPONS: None

THE *UNDICUR*-CLASS JUMPSPEEDER is generally used as an emergency vehicle. Produced by Kuat Vehicles before the Clone Wars, they are used by the Jedi, then by civilians during the time of the Empire. These jumpspeeders are quick, light, and easy to deploy, but they lack weapons and shields.

Simple controls

Sabine Wren pilots an *Undicur*-class jumpspeeder while fleeing Imperials on Lothal.

Padawan Rescue

A Force wielder known as "the Son" traps Obi-Wan Kenobi in a fiery volcano. Ahsoka Tano uses her jumpspeeder to help him escape.

Low-output repulsorlift engine

Small luggage capacity

Foot pedals

CONTROLS

Jumpspeeders fold up into a box-like shape. Pedal footpads control speed, while the altitude controls are located on handlebars.

MANDALORIAN SPEEDER

BALUTAR-CLASS SWOOP

MANUFACTURED ON MANDALORE, the *Balutar*-class swoop is an easy-to-fly speeder bike with a powerful engine. It is designed with the center of gravity directly beneath the pilot for faster response times.

DATA FILE

TYPE: Repulsorcraft
MANUFACTURER: MandalMotors
MODEL: *Balutar*-class swoop
LENGTH: 2.6 m (8 ft 6 in)
WEAPONS: None

Duchess Satine Kryze

POWER UP

The swoop's power generator is built into the front section. It can be adapted for patrol duty with the addition of twin blaster cannons.

Storage compartment

Airscoop

Pedal controls

Need for Speed

Obi-Wan Kenobi and Duchess Satine Kryze ride a Mandalorian speeder on Mandalore as they try to escape the planet's super commando troops.

The Mandalorian splinter group Death Watch uses *Balutar*-class swoops on the snowy Outer Rim world of Carlac.

STARHAWK SPEEDER

CIVILIAN STALWART

FAST, UPGRADEABLE, and easy to drive, this non-military speeder is also very affordable on the second-hand market. No wonder it is one of the most popular models of speeder in the galaxy!

Obi-Wan Kenobi and the pirate Hondo Ohnaka ride into the sulfur deserts of Florrum, on the hunt for Darth Maul's downed ship.

DATA FILE

TYPE: Repulsorcraft
MANUFACTURER: Ikas-Adno
SPEED: 665 kph (414 mph)
MODEL: Speeder bike
LENGTH: 3.4 m (13 ft 1 in)
WEAPONS: Available with 1 medium blaster cannon or 2 light blasters

EASY RIDER

Multiple sensors built into the front tip of the speeder guarantee a smooth ride, while rear stabilizers give it exceptional balance.

Passenger seat

Sidecar on some models

Custom paintwork

Stabilizer ski

Biker Gang

Turk Falso leads members of Hondo Ohnaka's Weequay pirate gang into battle with clones led by Commander Stone and Jar Jar Binks.

NIGHTSISTER SPEEDER

DATA FILE

TYPE: Repulsorcraft
MANUFACTURER: Ubrikkian Transports
SPEED: 650 kph (404 mph)
MODEL: Speeder bike
LENGTH: 5.8 m (19 ft)
WEAPONS: 2 heavy blaster cannons, 2 laser cannons

THIS NIGHTSISTER CRAFT IS an unusual variation on speeder bike design. Used by the mysterious Nightsisters of Dathomir, it features an angular engine and a passenger pod, both branching off a central pilot's pod. Little is known about it—the Nightsisters rarely share their secrets.

Asajj Ventress travels in a Nightsister speeder across Dathomir to the village of the Nightbrothers.

BUILT FOR TWO

Heavy armor protects the Nightsister speeder. Dual controls allow a passenger to take over in an emergency.

Armored engine

Passenger carriage

Savage Selected

When the Nightsister Asajj Ventress chooses Savage Opress to become a living weapon, she takes him away from his village in a Nightsister speeder.

Asajj Ventress

Foothold

Sensor array

74-Z SPEEDER BIKE

SCOUT SPEEDER

DATA FILE

TYPE: Repulsorcraft
MANUFACTURER: Aratech
Repulsor Company
SPEED: 500 kph (310 mph)
MODEL: Speeder bike
LENGTH: 3.3 m (10 ft 10 in)
WEAPONS: Blaster cannon

THE 74-Z SPEEDER IS the Imperial standard for speeders, and is most often used by specialized scout troopers. Stripped of all excess weight, it offers virtually no protection for its driver, but is capable of high speeds.

An earlier model of speeder, the 614-AvA, is a common sight on Imperial-controlled worlds such as Lothal.

Scout trooper

COMPLETE CONTROL

The speeder bike's steering and blaster cannon are controlled with a pair of handlebars. Its speed and altitude are maintained using the two foot pedals.

Maneuver controls

Steering vanes

Blaster cannon

Repulsorlift engine

Forest Chase

On the forest moon of Endor, Leia Organa and Luke Skywalker steal a 74-Z. They use their speeders to chase fleeing Imperial scouts.

JOBEN T-85 SPEEDER

LIMITED-EDITION BIKE

DATA FILE

TYPE: Repulsorcraft
MANUFACTURER: Zebulon Dak Speeder Corporation
SPEED: 475 kph (295 mph)
MODEL: Speeder bike
LENGTH: 2.4 m (7 ft 10 in)
WEAPONS: EMP emitter

A POWERFUL, LOW-RIDING SPEEDER with a sleek design, the Joben T-85 is named for famous swoop racer Thall Joben. The T-85 is highly prized among speeder bike enthusiasts as it is produced in a limited volume, and each one is engraved with Joben's signature.

Kanan Jarrus

Brake

Moll K-19 power generator

Dusat EMP emitter

BEAM POWER

The rear of the Joben T-85 is equipped with a tractor beam. Its double-battery system is fed by solar energy.

Trick Cyclist

On the planet Lothal, Kanan Jarrus shows off his riding skills by flipping backward in the seat of his T-85 and shooting at the stormtroopers that are pursuing him.

Steering fin

Ezra and Kanan ride a T-85 speeder into the Attolon wastes in search of the Force-sensitive Bendu.

37

REY'S SPEEDER

DESERT TRANSPORT

DATA FILE

TYPE: Repulsorcraft
MANUFACTURER: Custom
SPEED: 420 kph (261 mph)
MODEL: Speeder bike
LENGTH: 3.7 m (12 ft 2 in)
WEAPONS: None

THIS BULKY SPEEDER is truly one of a kind. It is custom-built from scavenged parts that Rey has found in the Starship Graveyard on Jakku. Its repulsorlifts, for example, are taken from the wreckage of downed X-wings.

Rey's speeder can haul heavy salvage, but mostly carries small items in loose nets.

Heat exchange vent

Rey's salvage bag

Pilot's seat

Stabilizer vane

Steering exhaust nozzles

LOAD OF HOT AIR

A vent on the top of Rey's speeder expels heat, while the large grille on the front serves as an air intake.

Personal Touch

Rey's speeder is equipped with a rider interface. This means that the speeder won't start without a valid fingerprint. Rey is the only one who can ride it!

LANDSPEEDERS

PERSONAL REPULSORCRAFT

LANDSPEEDERS ARE CHEAP and fast, which makes them popular for short journeys. They use repulsor technology to hover just above the ground, but cannot rise to any great height. Some models can be unreliable and need a lot of maintenance.

Turbine engine

Ezra Bridger and Kanan Jarrus use a landspeeder for transport on their way to train Sabine Wren in lightsaber combat.

Windshield

Repulsor cooling vents

Getaway Car

The RGC-18 landspeeder is popular on the planet Lothal. A gang of rebels use one to escape from an Imperial complex there.

FAST FASHION

Most landspeeders quickly lose their value when newer models go on sale. Ten years into the Empire's reign, the V-35 courier speeder is a cheap model, often found on Outer Rim planets like Lothal and Tatooine.

GIAN SPEEDER

ROYAL GUARD VEHICLE

GIAN SPEEDERS ARE COMMON on wealthy worlds and see action during the Invasion of Naboo. Many years later, they are used by the Resistance for patrols. Mechanics constantly work to maintain them, as by this point they are extremely outdated.

The Naboo Royal Guard's vehicle of choice is the Gian Speeder. They are mainly used for crowd control.

EXTRA PROTECTION

The Gian speeder's medium-grade hull plating and reinforced armor make it very resilient. Each laser cannon has its own power unit, allowing it to operate even if the speeder's main power generator is damaged.

Enlarged protective windshield

Cockpit can hold a pilot, gunner, and two passengers

Streamlined thrusters

Side-mounted laser cannon

Droid Blast

In an emergency, Gian speeders can be mounted with heavy-strike cannons. They are used to fire on Trade Federation AATs during the Battle of Naboo.

CLONE SWAMP SPEEDER

INFANTRY SUPPORT PLATFORM SPEEDER

DATA FILE

TYPE: Repulsorcraft
MANUFACTURER: Uulshos Manufacturing
SPEED: 100 kph (62 mph)
MODEL: ISP
LENGTH: 5 m (16 ft 5 in)
WEAPONS: 2 twin blaster cannons

THE ISP SPEEDER IS a repulsor-powered platform designed for patrolling swampy regions. This leads to it being nicknamed the "swamp speeder" by clone troopers. Built from the foundation of a standard BARC speeder, it can operate on almost any terrain, which makes it useful in a range of combat scenarios.

Housing for rear mounted turbofan

Right-hand pilot's seat

Repulsorlift

Swiveling twin blaster cannons

STRONG SPEEDER

The speeder relies upon its mighty turbofan and repulsors to move quickly and smoothly over the battlefield. Its powerful twin blaster cannons can disable much larger vehicles.

Scouting Ahead

During the last Battle of Felucia, clones patrol sectors of the planet in swamp speeders. They are on the lookout for any sign of droids.

Clone troopers use swamp speeders while battling the Separatist forces on Kashyyyk. These vehicles help the soldiers repel the larger siege vehicles of the droid army.

MANDALORIAN POLICE SPEEDER

BUIRK'ALOR-CLASS SPEEDER

DATA FILE

TYPE: Speeder
MANUFACTURER: MandalMotors
SPEED: 280 kph (174 mph)
MODEL: *Buirk'alor*-class
LENGTH: 10.1 m (33 ft 1 in)
WEAPONS: None

LAW ENFORCEMENT ON Mandalore is the job of the Mandalorian Guard. Its officers travel in these small, enclosed speeders, which can often be seen on patrol in the skylanes of the planet's domed capital city, Sundari. They have flashing emergency lights on top and prominent police markings on all sides.

The Mandalorian guard is dedicated to safety and security of all citizens. Members are recruited from every Mandalorian clan.

Emergency lights

Wraparound viewport

Mandalorian Guard emblem

Gull-wing door

"Police" in the Mando'a language

POLICE, OPEN UP!

The speeder's front and back viewports slide apart for access, with a pair of gull-wing doors lifting up to admit the pilot and up to three passengers.

Tea Trouble

When poisoned tea makes several Sundari children ill, Mandalore's leader, Duchess Satine Kryze, investigates. She is able to acquire a police speeder for her work.

LUKE'S LANDSPEEDER

X-34 LANDSPEEDER

DATA FILE

TYPE: Speeder
MANUFACTURER: SoroSuub Corporation
SPEED: 250 kph (155 mph)
MODEL: X-34
LENGTH: 3.4 m (11 ft 1 in)
WEAPONS: None

LUKE SKYWALKER'S X-34 landspeeder is used heavily over the years. Unsurprisingly, it gradually undergoes many repairs and small modifications, which set it apart from a factory model X-34. Despite this, the vehicle is not worth much—most people prefer newer models.

Luke uses his X-34 landspeeder to race across the deserts of Tatooine. He must find R2-D2 before his uncle discovers the droid is missing.

Thrust turbine

OLD RIDE

There are signs of wear and tear on Luke's speeder. it is missing the cowling for one of its turbines, has some dents, and is in need of a new paint job. Before leaving Tatooine, Luke still manages to sell the vehicle for 2,000 credits.

Repulsor vent grilles

Dent from racing

No Time to Lose

When Luke realizes his aunt and uncle are in danger, he rushes home in his landspeeder. Unfortunately, he is too late to save them from being destroyed by Imperial stormtroopers.

CANTO BIGHT POLICE SPEEDER

JET-STICK PATROL CRAFT

DATA FILE

TYPE: Repulsorlift craft
MANUFACTURER: Trochiliad Motors
MODEL: Zephyr GB-134
LENGTH: 2.98 m (9 ft 9 in)
WEAPONS: 2 anti-personnel laser cannons

THE NARROW, WINDING STREETS of Canto Bight's Old Town are no place for cumbersome speeders. Instead, the Canto Bight Police Department uses nimble craft known as jet-sticks to keep the peace and chase after troublemakers. Most criminals quickly realize that trying to run from a jet-stick is a waste of time.

Repulsor generating frame

Operator pylon

Police Headquarters

The Canto Bight Police Department (CBPD) headquarters is also the main base for the force's jet-stick vehicles. From here they can quickly reach the site of any trouble.

Maneuvering repulsors

Laser cannon

As Finn and Rose discover, the Canto Bight Police Department takes trespassing very seriously.

TIGHT CORNERS

Before its artificial sea was constructed, Canto Bight was an ancient city in the middle of a desert. Small, agile jet-sticks are perfect for the cramped alleyways that snake through the Old Town.

SKI SPEEDER

V-4X-D

DATA FILE

TYPE: Low-altitude repulsorcraft
MANUFACTURER: Roche Machines
MODEL: V-4X-D ski speeder
WIDTH: 11.5 m (37 ft 9 in)
WEAPONS: 2 medium laser cannons

THESE RUSTY-LOOKING CRAFT were once high-speed sports vehicles. Bought by cash-strapped rebels and turned into simple patrol speeders, they were then left to decay on the planet Crait. Decades later, they are all that separates the Resistance from certain defeat.

In a desperate move, a squadron of rickety ski speeders led by Poe Dameron charges at the First Order army on Crait.

Heat exchanger

Thrust vector ring

Open cockpit

Medium laser cannon

SKIING INTO BATTLE
The ski speeder is kept stable by a large ski, known as a halofoil, that extends from the vehicle into the ground. On Crait, the ski digs through the white salt surface and throws up red dust from the crystals beneath.

Desperate Deserter
Finn was trained to pilot speeders when he was a First Order stormtrooper. He now uses that training to battle his former allies.

45

MTT

MULTI-TROOP TRANSPORT

DATA FILE

TYPE: Repulsorcraft
MANUFACTURER:
Baktoid Armor Workshop
SPEED: 31 kph (19 mph)
MODEL: Multi-Troop
Transport
LENGTH: 31 m (101 ft 8 in)
WEAPONS: 2 twin blaster
cannons

THIS LUMBERING TROOP TRANSPORT is packed with 112 battle droids, and is used by the Trade Federation in its invasion of Naboo. Its droid cargo is inactive, but can be woken in seconds by a signal from a Droid Control Ship overhead. Later versions of the MTTs carry autonomous Separatist droids during the Clone Wars.

Separatist insignia

NOW IN COLOR

Trade Federation MTTs are a rusty brown color, while the later Separatist versions are usually painted white and blue. Some of these later models are adapted to carry super battle droids.

Main troop deployment hatch

Twin blaster cannon

Heavy-duty repulsor

Transport Transporter

When the Trade Federation invades Naboo, it transports its fleet of MTTs in the hangar bays of an enormous battleship. Their advance is halted only when the Droid Control Ship is destroyed, stopping the droids from moving.

The Jedi General Mace Windu has to contend with Separatist MTTs in the battle for control of the planet Ryloth.

AAT BATTLE TANK

ARMORED ASSAULT TANK

DATA FILE

TYPE: Repulsorlift vehicle
MANUFACTURER: Baktoid Armor Workshop
SPEED: 55 kph (34 mph)
MODEL: AAT-1
LENGTH: 9.75 m (32 ft)
WEAPONS: 1 heavy laser cannon, 2 lateral range-finding lasers, 6 energy shell projectile launchers, 2 lateral antipersonnel lasers

THE ARMORED ASSAULT TANK figures prominently during the Trade Federation's invasion of Naboo. Although the invasion fails, the formidable AAT is considered a huge success, and it becomes a key component of Separatist forces.

Heavy laser cannon

Front hatch

Lateral antipersonnel lasers

Energy shell projectile launchers

EASY ACCESS

The AAT main compartment can be accessed by a front-facing hatch or a rear exit ramp. The tank commander's compartment is separate from the rest of the tank interior.

Training

Captured AAT come in handy during Saw Gerrera's resistance training on the planet Onderon—a world controlled by Separatists.

During the Invasion of Naboo, AATs fire upon the energy shield protecting the Gungan Grand Army.

DEFOLIATOR TANK

DEFOLIATOR DEPLOYMENT TANK / DDT

THIS MODIFIED TANK IS capable of destroying organic life without damaging nearby buildings or machines. It launches biological warheads from a special defoliator cannon designed by the Separatist general Lok Durd.

DATA FILE

TYPE: Tank
MANUFACTURER: Lok Durd
SPEED: 55 kph (34 mph)
MODEL: Modified Armored Assault Tank
LENGTH: 12.5 m (41 ft)
WEAPONS: Turret-mounted defoliator missile launcher, 6 energy shell launchers, 2 range-finding lasers, 2 antipersonnel lasers

Separatist cyborg General Grievous orders a defoliator strike against the Nightsisters on the planet Dathomir.

Defoliator cannon

Range-finding laser

FOR FOUR

Each DDT requires four battle droids to function: one pilot, one gunner, and a pair of defoliator missile loaders.

Repulsorlift cowl

Energy shell launch tube

Preserved Village

When the DDT is tested on the planet Maridun, Jedi Knight Anakin Skywalker uses an energy shield to save the target village from its devastating effects.

48

SUPER TANK

DATA FILE

TYPE: Repulsorcraft
MANUFACTURER: Baktoid
Armor Workshop
SPEED: 40 kph (25 mph)
MODEL: Super tank
LENGTH: 12.6 m (41 ft 4 in)
WEAPONS: 2 twin
blaster cannons,
2 twin laser
cannon turrets,
concealed twin
warhead
launchers

DESPERATE TO REGAIN GROUND, the Separatists develop a new form of battle craft—experimental super tanks with ray shielding. They are virtually unstoppable, with no known weapon able to penetrate their defenses.

Twin warhead launchers

HEAVY DUTY

Heavy armor and ray-shielding technology make the super tank slow but sturdy. Some of the armor plating retracts to reveal twin warhead launchers.

Twin blaster cannon

Confederacy of Independent Systems logo

No Way Out

Jedi Knight Anakin Skywalker is pinned down by an overwhelming force of super tanks during an attack on the Separatists' weapons factory on the planet Geonosis.

Twin laser cannon turret

A super tank under the control of Jedi Padawans Barriss Offee and Ahsoka Tano destroys the weapons factory on Geonosis from the inside.

STUN TANK

MOBILE ION CANNON

THIS REPUBLIC TANK IS primarily an anti-aircraft weapon. Its ion cannon drains energy from the ships it targets, leaving them helpless. Despite being designed for use against droid vehicles, the tank sees little use during the Clone Wars.

TURBOLASER TECH

The design of the stun tank is an extension of technology used in the much larger SPHA-T. Stun tanks are deployed by the Republic in the Battle of Malastare, and are twice used to incapacitate the enormous Zillo Beast—once on Malastare and then on Coruscant.

Ion cannon

Viewport

Heavily
armored hull

Stun tanks must be used with care to avoid bringing down ships on your own position.

Ion Giant

When the Zillo Beast rises from the depths of Malastare, Anakin Skywalker orders stun tanks to blast it with ion energy. Eventually, sustained fire subdues the giant creature.

PIRATE TANK

POPULAR WITH PIRATES IN the most lawless parts of the galaxy, the WLO-5 speeder tank is powerful and easy to drive. Criminals use it to defend their strongholds from rivals and to attack those weaker than themselves.

DATA FILE

TYPE: Repulsorcraft
MANUFACTURER: Ubrikkian Ord Pedrova
SPEED: 110 kph (68 mph)
MODEL: WLO-5
LENGTH: 11.4 m (37 ft 4 in)
WEAPONS: Laser cannon, antipersonnel blasters

TANK TOP
There is room for pilots and troops inside the tank, with only the gunner up top. Most pirates choose to ride in the open, where they can look intimidating!

During the Clone Wars, the pirate Hondo Ohnaka uses speeder tanks in a show of force against hostage negotiator Jar Jar Binks.

Laser cannon

Antipersonnel blasters

Turbine engine

Steering vane

Armor plating

Repulsor cooling vents

Theft on Felucia
Hondo demands that a village hand over their valuable nysillin crop. Luckily, a group of Jedi and bounty hunters are ready to stop the pirates.

UMBARAN HOVER TANK

ADVANCED ASSAULT VEHICLE

THIS UNUSUAL TANK IS a clear example of how much Umbaran design differs from that of other species. Using technology far beyond the galactic standard, the Umbarans build weapons of war that are unpredictable and devastating.

DATA FILE

TYPE: Repulsorcraft
MANUFACTURER:
Ghost Armaments
MODEL: Umbaran
hover tank
LENGTH: 13 m (42 ft 7 in)
WEAPONS:
2 electromagnetic
plasma cannons

Plasma cannon

LETHAL LEGS
The hover tank's two plasma cannons can unleash massive energy bursts. They rotate to serve as landing struts when the vehicle is powered down.

Plasma
build-up

Cockpit

Plasma-
conducting
vane

Rotating
joint

Long-Range Risk
Reckless Jedi General Pong Krell leads the Republic's clone army along a main city road in the Battle of Umbara. This leaves the troops highly vulnerable to long-range strikes by hover tanks.

Hover tanks are susceptible to AT-RT fire, and several are destroyed by Republic forces in the early stages of the Battle of Umbara.

IMPERIAL TROOP TRANSPORT

GROUND ASSAULT VEHICLE

DATA FILE

TYPE: Repulsorcraft
MANUFACTURER: Ubrikkian Industries
SPEED: 150 kph (93 mph)
MODEL: K79-S80
LENGTH: 8.7 m (28 ft 6 in)
WEAPONS: 2 laser guns, 1 twin laser turret

THE ITT'S MAIN FUNCTION is to deliver stormtroopers into battle, but it can be used to detain and transport prisoners, too. It is also designed to ferry supplies on its flat roof and sides, and this flexibility makes it a common sight on worlds recently occupied by Imperial forces.

BE PREPARED

The ITT is not designed as a combat ship, but it is equipped with two forward laser guns and a rear twin laser turret to defend itself in the event of an attack.

Viewport

Forward laser

Cargo racks

Imperial combat driver

Rack and Ruin

After a convoy of troop transports attacks a farming outpost on Lothal, the outpost's inhabitants are captured by stormtroopers and imprisoned in the ITT cargo racks.

The young Ezra Bridger is caught in the act while trying to steal a cargo of meiloorun fruit from an ITT on the planet Lothal.

KHETANNA

JABBA THE HUTT'S SAIL BARGE

DATA FILE

TYPE: Repulsorcraft
MANUFACTURER:
Ubrikkian Industries
SPEED: 100 kph (62 mph)
MODEL: Modified
sail barge
LENGTH: 30 m (98 ft 5 in)
WEAPONS: Laser cannon

THE CRIME LORD Jabba the Hutt travels across the Dune Sea of Tatooine in this modified luxury sail barge. It is powered by a repulsorlift engine, but can also use its sails to slowly move by wind power. Inside, it is equipped with all the luxuries Jabba needs to impress his fellow crooks.

ARMED BARGE

The *Khetanna* is designed purely as a pleasure barge, and has been modified to suit the needs of a gangster Hutt. It boasts fittings for heavy blasters, and has a powerful laser cannon on deck.

Forward sail

Lead lookout point

Decorative armor plating

Steering vane

Repulsor engine cooling vents

Nasty Hutt

Jabba travels in the *Khetanna* to the Great Pit of Carkoon. He intends to watch Luke Skywalker, Han Solo, and Chewbacca being fed to the Sarlacc that resides in the Great Pit.

Jabba the Hutt meets a violent end aboard the *Khetanna* at the hands of his prisoner, Leia Organa.

DESERT SKIFF

BANTHA-II CARGO SKIFF

DATA FILE

TYPE: Repulsorcraft
MANUFACTURER:
Ubrikkian Industries
SPEED: 250 kph (155 mph)
MODEL: Bantha-II
cargo skiff
LENGTH: 9.5 m (31 ft 2 in)
WEAPONS: None fitted
as standard

CHEAP AND BASIC, small desert skiffs are a common sight on planets where resources are limited. The Bantha-II skiff is a favorite of gangsters and pirates, who use the vessels for raids, patrols, and prisoner escorts.

Luke Skywalker battles Jabba the Hutt's henchmen on a skiff hovering above the deadly Great Pit of Carkoon.

Control column

Forward lookout

Steering vane

Repulsor drive

SHIPS OF THE DESERT

Skiffs have proven particularly useful on the many desert worlds of the Outer Rim. They are popular with the Weequay gangs that hunt for treasure on worlds such as Jakku and Ponemah.

Pirate Plank

Standard skiff design is simple and easily customizable. The Tatooine crime lord Jabba the Hutt has one of his skiffs outfitted with a gangplank to indulge his cruel tendencies.

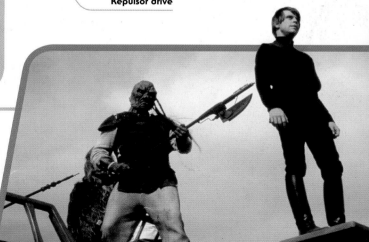

SPIDER DROID

OG-9 HOMING SPIDER DROID

DATA FILE

TYPE: Walker
MANUFACTURER: Baktoid Armor Workshop
SPEED: 90 kph (56 mph)
MODEL: OG-9 homing spider droid
HEIGHT: 7.3 m (23 ft 11 in)
WEAPONS: Top and bottom laser cannons

THE OG-9 IS A WALKING TANK with a droid brain, and is one of the most terrifying weapons in the Separatist armory. Designed for massive ground assaults, its top-mounted laser emplacement breaks down enemy deflector shields while its lower laser cannon keeps attacking infantry at bay.

FOUR LEGS GOOD

The thin legs of a spider droid are tougher than they look, and can take on any terrain. But only one leg needs to be disabled to bring the whole droid tumbling down.

Laser cannon

Droid "eye"

Armored reactor core

Hydraulic leg

All-terrain footpad

Spider droids advance alongside AATs on the jungle world of Felucia.

Giant Spider

Spider droids tower over their fellow battle droids in the Battle of Geonosis. This is the first engagement of what would come to be known as the Clone Wars.

DWARF SPIDER DROID

DSD1 DWARF SPIDER DROID

DATA FILE

TYPE: Battle droid
MANUFACTURER: Baktoid
Armor Workshop
SPEED: 90 kph (56 mph)
MODEL: DSD1
HEIGHT: 1.9 m (6 ft 2 in)
without antenna
WEAPONS: Laser cannon

A WALKING CANNON WITH a droid brain, the DSD1 is designed to take on enemies in confined spaces. However, during the Clone Wars the droid is deployed on open battlefields alongside larger equivalents such as the OG-9 homing spider droid.

Tracing antenna

Infrared photoreceptor

During the Battle of Kashyyyk, dwarf spider droids emerge from the sea. They target Republic vehicles with their laser cannons.

Armored droid brain casing

Articulated legs

Laser cannon

Cut Down to Size
Dwarf spider droids are no match for a Jedi Knight. Anakin Skywalker proves this during a lightsaber ambush in the Second Battle of Felucia.

FIRE IN THE BELLY
Each dwarf spider droid has a weak spot on its belly that makes it vulnerable to well-placed explosives. They can also blow themselves up in battle, using their self-destruct devices as a weapon.

SPHA-T

SELF-PROPELLED HEAVY ARTILLERY TURBOLASER

DATA FILE

TYPE: Heavy artillery
MANUFACTURER: Rothana
Heavy Engineering
SPEED: 35 kph (22 mph)
MODEL: Self-Propelled
Heavy Artillery Turbolaser
LENGTH: 140.2 m (459 ft
11 in)
WEAPONS: Heavy turbolaser

BEARING ONE OF THE bigger ground guns used by the Republic Army, this 12-legged walker is a slow but steady feature throughout the Clone Wars. Its turbolaser can destroy a starship, but can only operate for a limited time. This is because each blast uses up a vast amount of energy.

SPHA-Ts are usually deployed in groups, co-ordinating their fire for maximum destructive effect.

Turbolaser focus lens

Turbolaser barrel

Elevating mechanism

Infantry platform

Viewport

FATAL FLAW
The SPHA-T has a limited tracking mechanism due to the fixed nature of the main gun. It is eventually replaced with the much smaller and faster SPMA.

Heavily armored hull

Articulated low legs

Team Turbo
It takes a crew of 30 clone troopers to operate a SPHA-T. The gunners do not fire when the vehicle is in motion. Instead they rely on pilots to position the legs correctly before taking aim.

AT-TE

ALL TERRAIN TACTICAL ENFORCER

DATA FILE

TYPE: Walker
MANUFACTURER: Rothana
Heavy Engineering
SPEED: 60 kph (37 mph)
MODEL: All Terrain
Tactical Enforcer
LENGTH: 13.2 m (43 ft 4 in)
WEAPONS: 6 laser cannons,
1 mass driver cannon

THE AT-TE LOOKS MORE like a huge robotic insect than a military transport. It is used during the Clone Wars to move large numbers of troops through battle, and to operate as a mobile command center.

Retirement Home

During the rule of the Empire, clone troopers Rex, Wolffe, and Gregor live in an old AT-TE. It has sleeping bunks, ladders, and a kitchen. They even attach a fishing line to the cannon!

Mass driver cannon

Tough armor

Cockpit front
window

Laser cannon

Triple-jointed
hydraulic limbs

By striking from afar, the AT-TEs remove the energy shield protecting the weapons factory of Poggle the Lesser.

SPECIAL WALKER

The AT-TE is a force to be reckoned with. It is heavily shielded, and specially equipped versions can even scale high cliffs. Its magnetized feet also enable it to walk upside down on metal surfaces.

AT-OT

DATA FILE

TYPE: Walker
MANUFACTURER: Kuat
Drive Yards
SPEED: 55 kph (34 mph)
MODEL: All Terrain Open
Transport
LENGTH: 14.3 m (46 ft 11 in)
WEAPONS: 2 forward-
facing medium laser
cannons, 2 antipersonnel
rear laser cannons

THE IMPOSING AT-OT HAS an open-top design, leaving it vulnerable to attack from above. Their role during the Clone Wars is to quickly move troops, rather than engage in battle.

Clone troopers rely on AT-OTs during the Battle of Felucia. They use them to navigate the jungle landscape.

Rear laser cannon

Clone trooper seating

SMOOTH JOURNEY

AT-OTs are usually dropped well behind friendly lines. Their anti-gravity engines and a forward-facing fin ensure a stable ride.

Forward-
facing cannon

Heavy, five-toed
footpad

Trooper Ambush

The Jedi Aayla Secura is leading a squadron of clone troopers carried on AT-OTs at the time of her betrayal and execution.

AT-RT

ALL TERRAIN RECON TRANSPORT

DATA FILE

- **TYPE:** Walker
- **MANUFACTURER:** Kuat Drive Yards
- **SPEED:** 75 kph (47 mph)
- **MODEL:** All Terrain Recon Transport
- **HEIGHT:** 3.2 m (10 ft 6 in)
- **WEAPONS:** 1 laser cannon, 1 blaster cannon, 1 mortar launcher

FAST, NIMBLE, AND POWERFUL AT-RTs are used during the brutal land battles of the Clone Wars. A single clone trooper will usually pilot these as a scout, ranging ahead of the battlefront and gathering intel for the main force.

LONG DISTANCE
Each walker is equipped with advanced motion detection and sensor equipment. Its light build allows it to jump long distances.

Laser cannon

Charging In
AT-RTs are launched from the cargo bays of Low Altitude Assault Transports into the Battle of Umbara. They are defeated by the Umbarans' superior weaponry.

Powerful, articulated legs

Several AT-RTs are cut down while trying to charge enemy lines during the Battle of Christophsis.

AT-DP

DATA FILE

TYPE: Walker
MANUFACTURER: Kuat Drive Yards
SPEED: 90 kph (56 mph)
MODEL: All Terrain Defense Pod
HEIGHT: 11.6 m (38 ft)
WEAPONS: 1 heavy laser cannon

Pilot's viewport

Heavy laser cannon

Hip joint

AFTER THE SUCCESS OF the AT-RT walker during the Clone Wars, the Empire commissions a new and improved model—the AT-DP. This walker combines the mobility of the AT-RT with an armored cockpit to protect its two-person crew. It is used to maintain peace with a strong military presence.

UNSAFE ARMOR
While AT-DP may look sturdy, its armor cannot withstand a direct hit by a missile. Its pod has even been known to explode under heavy stress!

Jedi Control
In an attempt to rescue the notorious pirate Hondo Ohnaka from an Imperial prison, Jedi apprentice Ezra Bridger uses the Force to control the pilot of an AT-DP. He turns the walker against its own allies.

Cikatro Vizago flees his smuggler camp when an Imperial cruiser arrives carrying two AT-DPs.

AT-ST

ALL TERRAIN SCOUT TRANSPORT

Light blaster cannon

DATA FILE

TYPE: Walker
MANUFACTURER: Kuat Drive Yards
SPEED: 90 kph (56 mph)
MODEL: All Terrain Scout Transport
HEIGHT: 9 m (28 ft 3 in)
WEAPONS: Twin blaster cannon, concussion missiles, concussion grenades

THE AT-ST IS A VEHICLE used by the Empire. It moves quickly on even ground, and is capable of navigating difficult terrain. They are typically marched around captured territory as a show of force, and a symbol of the Empire's strength.

Leg joint

An AT-ST is deployed in Jedha City during a battle between Imperials and Saw Gerrera's rebels.

OLD MODEL

The AT-ST's design can be traced to earlier walker models. These vehicles included the AT-DP and the AT-RT, which was commonly used by the Republic during the Clone Wars.

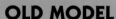
Computer-controlled foot sensor

The Battle of Endor

AT-STs are relied on heavily in the Battle of Endor. Rebel forces use several obvious design flaws to their own advantage.

AT-AT

ALL TERRAIN ARMORED TRANSPORT

THERE ARE FEW THINGS as terrifying as the sight of an AT-AT walking toward you. These weapons of destruction are used in the later years of the Empire's reign. The mere presence of one is usually enough to ensure obedience from any local resistance.

DATA FILE

TYPE: Walker
MANUFACTURER: Kuat Drive Yards
SPEED: 60 kph (37 mph)
MODEL: All Terrain Armored Transport
HEIGHT: 22.5 m (74 ft)
WEAPONS: 2 laser cannons, 2 medium blasters

Movable, heavily armed head

Hull with seating for troops

Side hatch

Sturdy footpad

Unusual Shelter

Rey lives as a scavenger on Jakku. Her home is inside the ruined remains of an AT-AT that was destroyed decades earlier.

The Empire uses AT-ATs against the Rebel Alliance during the invasion of Hoth.

THREE OPERATORS

A pilot, a gunner, and a commander operate the AT-AT. It can also carry up to 40 ground soldiers.

AT-ACT

ALL TERRAIN ARMORED CARGO TRANSPORT

Head-mounted sensor array

DATA FILE

TYPE: Walker
MANUFACTURER: Kuat Drive Yards
SPEED: 50 kph (31 mph)
MODEL: All Terrain Armored Cargo Transport
HEIGHT: 31.9 m (104 ft 8 in)
WEAPONS: 2 heavy laser cannons

THESE IMPERIAL WALKERS ARE not as dangerous as their huge size suggests. Balancing a large transport on such long, thin legs with joints held together by electromagnets makes these walkers highly unstable. They were originally built for haulage, not combat.

Drive motor

Hangar clamp notches

CONSTRUCTION WALKER

AT-ACTs are mainly used for hauling cargo for construction projects. However, in emergencies the walkers can also be deployed as military vehicles.

Knee joint cover

Under Fire

AT-ACTs can resist attack from most handheld weapons. However, they cannot survive a starfighter assault, and many AT-ACTs are destroyed by rebel ships during the Battle of Scarif.

When a band of rebels attacks Scarif, all Imperial defensive units are ordered into battle—even AT-ACTs and non-military personnel.

AT-M6

ALL TERRAIN MEGACALIBER SIX

DATA FILE

TYPE: Artillery walker
MANUFACTURER: Kuat-Entralla Drive Yards
MODEL: All Terrain MegaCaliber Six
HEIGHT: 36.18 m (118 ft 4 in)
WEAPONS: 1 MegaCaliber Six turbolaser cannon, 2 heavy laser cannons, 2 anti-ship laser cannons

THIS MASSIVE WAR MACHINE forms the core of the First Order's invasion army. Combining tough, heavy armor with devastating firepower, it is a terrifying opponent on any battlefield. Its huge front limbs give it the menacing appearance of a giant predator.

MegaCaliber Six turbolaser cannon

Armored cockpit

Turbolaser fuel cells

The AT-M6's name comes from the MegaCaliber Six cannon that it carries on its back. This enormous weapon can smash through the toughest durasteel armor.

BIG BROTHER

Although they look similar to AT-ATs, the First Order's AT-M6s are much larger than those earlier walkers.

Mecha-carpal foot structure

Line of Battle

A formation of AT-M6s lumbers toward the Resistance defenders on the barren world of Crait. These towering metal monsters are almost unstoppable.

GUNGAN BATTLE WAGON

DATA FILE

TYPE: Wheeled ammunition transport
MANUFACTURER: Gungan Grand Army
SPEED: 25 kph (16 mph)
MODEL: Wagon
LENGTH: 15 m (49 ft 3 in)
WEAPONS: None

THE GUNGAN ARMY rises up from the depths of its underwater home to liberate Naboo from the Trade Federation. In support of its larger artillery, the army makes use of battle wagons to haul volatile explosives, named boomas.

During the Battle of Naboo, Jar Jar Binks accidentally deploys a wagon of ammunition against the attacking droids.

Gungan cesta to defend cargo

Organically grown chassis

RELIABLE STEED

Battle wagons are hauled by creatures called falumpasets. These powerful mammals are stubborn but intelligent.

Gungan warrior

Large wheels

Back to Basics

The Gungan battle wagon is one of few land-based vehicles to use wheels instead of hovering above the ground.

HAILFIRE DROID

IG-227 *HAILFIRE*-CLASS DROID TANK

DATA FILE

TYPE: Droid tank
MANUFACTURER:
Haor Chall Engineering
SPEED: 45 kph (28 mph)
MODEL: IG-227
HEIGHT: 6.8 m (27 ft 10 in)
WEAPONS: 30 guided
missiles, twin chin-
mounted blasters

LESS A VEHICLE AND more a mobile missile platform, the IG-227 is a common sight on the battlefields in the earliest months of the Clone Wars. The droid-controlled vehicle is soon phased out, however: though powerful, the weapons platform simply cannot carry enough ammunition.

Hailfire droids roll into action on the planet Geonosis, alongside battle droids and super battle droids.

EYE ON THE SKY

Hailfire droids use a photoreceptor "eye" to home in on their targets from impressive distances. Their missiles follow deliberately unpredictable paths on the way to their targets, leaving a thick, black exhaust trail in their wake.

Unique, hoop-like wheels

Wheel of Fortune

The IG-227 is donated to the Separatist cause by San Hill's InterGalactic Banking Clan.

Missile pod

Photoreceptor

Sensors

CORPORATE ALLIANCE TANK DROID

NR-N99 *PERSUADER*-CLASS DROID ENFORCER

DATA FILE

TYPE: Droid tank
MANUFACTURER:
Techno Union
SPEED: 50 kph (31 mph)
MODEL: NR-N99
Persuader-class
LENGTH: 10.9 m
(35 ft 9 in)
WEAPONS: Ion cannons,
heavy repeating blasters,
missile launchers

SOMETIMES KNOWN AS THE snail tank, this rolling weapon is controlled by a built-in droid brain. The tank is developed for the Corporate Alliance to further its business interests by force. When the Corporate Alliance sides with the Separatists, the tank droid faces the Republic's clone troopers in battle.

Photoreceptor "eye"

Heavy repeating blaster

Heavy-duty track

In the Battle of Malastare, the Republic defeats battle droids, super battle droids, and tank droids alike with an electro-proton bomb.

ON TRACK

With its large central tread and smaller tracks on either side, the tank droid can take on almost any terrain with ease.

Brain Off

Though the tank droid is designed to function without a driver, it can also be controlled by a pilot battle droid. This is the case during the Battle of Kashyyyk.

WHEEL BIKE

TSMEU-6 PERSONAL WHEEL BIKE

DATA FILE

TYPE: Personal transport
MANUFACTURER:
Z-Gomot Ternbuell
Guppat Corporation
SPEED: 330 kph (205 mph)
MODEL: TSMEU-6
LENGTH: 3.5 m (11 ft 6 in)
WEAPONS: Heavy double
laser cannon

WHEEL BIKES ARE PRIMARILY designed for mining operations. However, as is often the case, these swift, sturdy, and agile vehicles have become popular on the second-hand market as modified weapons platforms. They are also favored by racing enthusiasts.

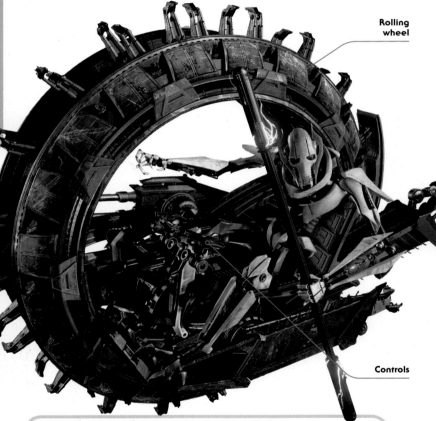

Rolling wheel

Heavy double laser cannon

Controls

FAST ROLLER

The seat and cannon of the wheel bike remain stable while the rest of the vehicle rotates vertically around the driver. It also houses four retractable legs, which allow the bike to navigate uneven terrain.

General Grevious removes the bike's passenger seat to accommodate his cannon.

Jedi Chase

During the final days of the Clone Wars, General Grievous tries to escape using a wheel bike. Obi-Wan Kenobi pursues the villain on the back of a reptilian varactyl named Boga.

CLONE TURBO TANK

HAVW A6 JUGGERNAUT

DATA FILE

TYPE: Tank
MANUFACTURER: Kuat Drive Yards
SPEED: 160 kph (99 mph)
MODEL: HAVw A6 Juggernaut
LENGTH: 49.4 m (162 ft)
WEAPONS: Antipersonnel cannons, heavy laser turret, projectile launchers, repeating laser

THIS 10-WHEELED TANK can deliver as many as 300 clone troopers into the heart of battle in one trip. It is designed to roll over any terrain with ease and to absorb enemy fire with no loss of function. After proving effective in the Clone Wars, the tank stays in use during the age of Empire.

Jedi Padawan Ahsoka Tano is taken prisoner by Trandoshan hunters during a turbo tank strike on the planet Felucia.

Repeating laser

Heavy laser turret

Antipersonnel laser cannon

Sturdy suspension

END TO END

The clone turbo tank has cockpits at both ends and can operate with either as the front. It also has a medical bay and storage areas for small support craft.

Final Battle

Turbo tanks play a large part in the defeat of the Separatists at the Battle of Kashyyyk. However the victory is hollow, as the clones turn against the Jedi.

IMPERIAL ASSAULT TANK

TX-225 OCCUPIER TANK

DATA FILE

TYPE: Ground assault vehicle/tank
MANUFACTURER: Rothana Heavy Engineering
SPEED: 72 kph (45 mph)
MODEL: TX-225 Occupier
LENGTH: 7.3 m (23 ft 11 in)
WEAPONS: 3 twin medium laser cannons

IMPERIAL TROOPS USE THESE ground assault vehicles to stay in control on rebellious worlds. They are slow, but surprisingly maneuverable in built-up areas. Each tank is heavily armed, with two rotating twin laser cannons and a third in a forward fixed position.

Occupier tanks inspire fear in the inhabitants of Jedha City, but also provoke daring acts of rebellion among them.

Armored cargo module

Twin medium laser cannon

Motive track

On Patrol

TX-225 Occupier tanks patrol the Holy City of Jedha. The driver and the commander look out from hatches, while the gunner/technician remains unseen.

TWO TANKS

The primary model of Occupier is the TX-225 GAVw, which runs on heavy metal tracks. An experimental version, the TX-225 GAVr uses repulsorlifts to hover.

SANDCRAWLER

MOBILE JAWA FORTRESS

DATA FILE

TYPE: Treaded ground transport
MANUFACTURER: Corellia Mining Corporation
SPEED: 30 kph (19 mph)
HEIGHT: 20 m (65 ft 7 in)
WEAPONS: None

SANDCRAWLERS ARE brought to Tatooine during a mining boom. When the mines are picked clean, the machinery is abandoned. The sandcrawlers are soon claimed by one of the few native races on the planet—the Jawas.

Jawas find R2-D2 and C-3PO in the Tatooine desert, and sell the droids to Owen Lars and his nephew, Luke Skywalker.

JAWA HOME

Each huge sandcrawler is home to an entire clan of hooded Jawa scavengers. They use sandcrawlers as mobile junkyards, trawling the vast deserts of the world for abandoned machinery that can be repaired and resold.

Cockpit

Power cell

Auxiliary forward hatch

Steerable front treads

Electrostatic repellers keep sand from interior components

A Helping Hand

The sight of a sandcrawler on Tatooine is usually a welcome one. Whether someone is hoping to buy or sell something, or just needs to ask for directions, Jawas are happy to help.

WATER

GONDOLA SPEEDER

BESPOKE SPEEDER

DATA FILE

TYPE: Luxury water craft
MANUFACTURER: Varykino Workshop
SPEED: 100 kph (62 mph)
MODEL: *Berenko*-class
LENGTH: 7.9 m (25 ft 11 in)
WEAPONS: None

THE HANDCRAFTED GONDOLA SPEEDER is created for the Naberrie family to use on the deep lakes of Naboo. Intended to be both aesthetically pleasing and environmentally friendly, these speeders are mainly used for pleasure.

Downthrusters housed in curved stern

WATER WORTHY

Repulsorlifts keep the gondola speeder just above the water. It can carry up to four people, and is equipped with emergency communicators and inflatable paddles.

Passenger seats

Hull houses engine

Joy Ride

Senator Padmé Amidala retreats to Naboo after someone threatens her life. While there, she journeys in a gondola speeder with her protector, Anakin Skywalker.

Several gondola speeders are kept in service at Varykino, the lake retreat of the Naberrie family.

NABOO WATER SPEEDER

LAKE COUNTRY PLEASURE CRAFT

DATA FILE

TYPE: Luxury water craft
MANUFACTURER: Theed Palace Engineering Corps
SPEED: 120 kph (75 mph)
MODEL: D-11 water speeder
LENGTH: 7 m (23 ft)
WEAPONS: None

THE SERENE LAKES OF NABOO are the planet's most famous sight, renowned across the galaxy for their peaceful vistas. In their free time, the Naboo take luxurious pleasure speeders out onto the water, exploring the hidden coves and majestic waterfalls.

FAMILY RESEMBLANCE

The D-11 is manufactured by the same company as the N-1 starfighter, and the two craft share many design features, despite being built to operate in very different environments.

Rear-facing passenger seats

Main drive turbines are designed to reduce noise

Rear-mounted repulsor generator

Tail based on N-1 starfighter

The royal boathouse is built into the base of the Theed cliffs. It is an ancient structure, used by many kings and queens of Naboo over the years.

Palace Craft

The D-11 water speeders were built specially for the use of the queen and the royal household. A section of the royal boathouse is set aside for their recharging and maintenance, however Padmé Amidala is less indulgent than some previous queens, and the D-11s are seldom used.

HUTT SWAMP SPEEDER

PONGEETA-CLASS SPEEDER

A MORE MODERN TAKE on traditional fanboats, *Pongeeta*-class speeders are a status symbol for wealthy Hutts. They are designed to float just above the swamps that cover most of the Hutt homeworld, Nal Hutta.

DATA FILE

TYPE: Repulsorcraft
MANUFACTURER:
Ubrikkian Industries
SPEED: 80 kph (50 mph)
MODEL: *Pongeeta*-class
LENGTH: 12.3 m (40 ft 4 in)
WEAPONS: None

OLD AND NEW

The swamp speeder swaps propeller fans for ion engines and repulsor technology. Steering is controlled by maneuvering two thrusters at the sides of the main engines.

Fan-style ion engine

Crime lord Ziro the Hutt

Traditional Hutt designs

Pressor-field generator

Sy Snootles at the controls

Passenger seating for humanoids

Flat platform for Hutt travelers

Swamp Swap

After escaping from a Hutt prison, the crime lord Ziro speeds into the depths of the swamp. He seeks out his mother so he can trade his speeder for her starship.

Bounty hunter Cad Bane follows Ziro through the swamps of Nal Hutta in a swamp speeder.

TRIBUBBLE BONGO

GUNGAN BONGO SUBMARINE

DATA FILE

TYPE: Submarine
MANUFACTURER: Otoh Gunga Bongmeken Cooperative
SPEED: 85 kph (53 mph)
MODEL: Tribubble bongo
LENGTH: 15 m (49 ft 2 in)
WEAPONS: None

THESE SEMI-ORGANIC submarines have hulls that are grown rather than built, so no two are exactly alike. The Gungans equip them with hydrostatic bubble shields to keep the air in and the water out, and use them to explore the oceans of their home planet, Naboo.

Gungan Jar Jar Binks takes Qui-Gon Jinn and Obi-Wan Kenobi to Naboo's capital city, Theed, in a bongo.

Port cargo bubble

Electromotive tentacles

IN A SPIN

The long, organic tentacles that flow from the back of the bongo spin to propel the vessel through water.

Cockpit bubble

Forward driving plane

A Bigger Fish

A bongo piloted by Obi-Wan is caught by a huge opee sea killer! It takes the arrival of an even bigger sea creature—the sando aqua monster—to save Obi-Wan's ship.

KAMINO SUBMARINE

AQUATIC TRANSPORT

DATA FILE

TYPE: Submarine
MANUFACTURER: Kamino Engineering
SPEED: 140 kph (87 mph)
MODEL: KE-UW33
LENGTH: 7.3 m (23 ft 11 in)
WEAPONS: None

BUILT TO EXPLORE THE watery depths of Kamino, these submarines can withstand the pressures of even the deepest ocean. Since Kamino's seas do not have any hostile creatures, the submarines are not equipped with weapons.

Emergency escape system in cockpit

Tail lights

Air filtration vents

UNDERWATER

The Kamino submarine can carry only one person. It comes with a life pod that can separate from the craft in an emergency. Its bright lights penetrate even the darkest ocean depths.

Suspicious Findings

When Separatists attack Kamino, Obi-Wan Kenobi believes that the debris crashing into the ocean are suspicious. He borrows a Kamino sub to investigate.

Intense beam headlights for visibility

Obi-Wan is forced to abandon his submarine when it comes under attack from aqua droids.

OMS DEVILFISH SUB

ONE MAN SUBMERSIBLE DEVILFISH

DATA FILE

TYPE: Submarine
MANUFACTURER: Kuat Drive Yards
SPEED: 40 kph (24.9 mph)
MODEL: OMS Devilfish
LENGTH: 2.43 m (7 ft 11 in)
WEAPONS: 2 blaster cannons, 2 laser cannons

THE OMS DEVILFISH SUB provides soldiers with a fast way to move through underwarer environments. There are many different types of one man submarines used by civilians, but the Devilfish is the vehicle of choice for the Grand Army of the Republic.

Weapon control handgrips

CIVIL WAR

When the Quarrens of Mon Cala side with the Separatist Alliance, the Mon Calamari are forced to use the Devilfish subs against their aquatic cousins.

Dual blaster cannon

Propulsion jet

Laser cannons

When Anakin Skywalker loses his helmet, he quickly runs out of air! Luckily, Ahsoka uses a Devilfish to recover and return his helmet in time.

Ready to Ride

Kit Fisto and Ahsoka Tano lead clone troopers into the oceans of Mon Cala. They jump aboard Republic-commissioned Devilfish submarines to reach the underwater battle faster.

81

QUARREN UTS PIKE

UNDERWATER TURBO SLED PIKE

DATA FILE

TYPE: Submarine
MANUFACTURER: QiuQin Inc.
SPEED: 50 kph (31 mph)
MODEL: Underwater Turbo Sled Pike
LENGTH: 1.8 m (5 ft 11 in)
WEAPONS: Dual blaster cannon, ink cloud

THESE MILITARY SUBMARINES ARE built in secret by the Quarren Isolation League on the ocean world of Mon Cala. They are considered illegal by the planet's ruling Mon Calamari elite, which controls a military with better-armed but slower submersibles of its own.

Propulsion system

Underwater War

During the Clone Wars, the Quarren Isolation League stage a coup against the Mon Calamari. The Separatists send an army of aqua droids to fight beside the Quarren.

Defensive spikes

When Republic forces arrive to reinforce the Mon Calamari, Jedi Master Kit Fisto takes on several Quarren Isolation League soldiers and seizes a UTS Pike for his own use.

ADDED EXTRA

The Quarren are strong swimmers who can breathe underwater, so do not need submarines. However, a UTS Pike gives its user extra speed and offensive capabilities.

Blaster cannon

TRIDENT-CLASS ASSAULT SHIP

DRILL ASSAULT CRAFT

DATA FILE

TYPE: Assault ship
MANUFACTURER: Colicoid
Creation Nest
MODEL: *Trident*-class
LENGTH: 88.7 m (291 ft)
HYPERDRIVE: None
WEAPONS: 8 laser cannons,
1 drill spike

THESE TENTACLED SHIPS ARE heavily shielded and even more heavily armed. With their four tentacles acting as both a means of mobility and as weapons, the *Trident*-class ships serve as devastating war machines whether on land or in water.

During a battle with the Mon Calamari, Karkarodon leader Riff Tamson uses a *Trident*-class vessel as his command ship.

Observation portal

Durasteel, mechanical tentacles

Drill to penetrate battleship hulls

Magnetic grapples

City Assault

Trident-class ships are secretly deployed in the oceans of Kamino. They attack Tipoca City, the medical and bioengineering facility where new clones are created and trained.

TENTACLED TERROR

The *Trident*-class ship is a formidable vessel. Its drill spike is used to break through ship hulls, and its tentacles are built with powerful magnetic grapples. The "head" of the ship can carry several Separatist droids, ready to be deployed into battle.

SPACE

ESCAPE PODS

EMERGENCY LIFE RAFTS

SMALL EMERGENCY CRAFT are fitted as standard on most large, deep-space vehicles. While the design and features of these pods vary greatly from ship to ship, they all share a single purpose—to save lives.

DATA FILE

TYPE: Varies
MANUFACTURER: Various
SPEED: Varies
MODEL: Varies
LENGTH: Typically around 10 m (32 ft 9 in)
HYPERDRIVE: Varies
WEAPONS: Rarely

OFF WORLD

Some planets have a supply of homemade escape pods to carry a person to safety in an emergency. When Order 66 turns the clone troopers against the Jedi, Yoda uses an escape pod to get away from Kashyyyk.

Short-range main thrusters

Altitude-control thruster

Pod from a Republic ship

Viewport

Abandon Ship!

When Separatists led by General Grievous board a Republic ship, Obi-Wan Kenobi launches its self-destruct sequence. The Jedi and his crew then abandon the vessel in escape pods.

Droids R2-D2 and C-3PO use an escape pod to flee the *Tantive IV* when it is boarded by Darth Vader's troops. It lands on the nearest planet: Tatooine.

DROCH-CLASS BOARDING SHIP

SEPARATIST POD-HUNTER

DATA FILE

TYPE: Boarding ship
MANUFACTURER: Colicoid
Creation
SPEED: 850 kph (528 mph)
MODEL: Droch-class
LENGTH: 18.5 m (60 ft 8 in)
HYPERDRIVE: None
WEAPONS: Light laser
cannons

Holding
area hatch

THE *DROCH*-CLASS BOARDING
ships are Separatist weapons.
They are designed to pierce
the hulls of ships or
buildings. This allows the
troops inside to attack
enemies unexpectedly,
and capture ships without
destroying them.

Propulsion vent

Light laser cannon

SEEK AND FIND
Each *Droch*-class boarding
ship carries one pilot and
six battle droids. It comes
with claws that retract during
travel, and has lights on
the hull that can be used
to search through debris.

Retracting
pincer claw

Pod-Hunters
These boarding
ships are used to
hunt down Republic
escape pods during
the Battle of Abregado.

A *Droch*-class ship lands on
the Republic base on the
Rishi moon. It unleashes a
squad of droid commandos
to take over the base.

TACTICAL INFILTRATION POD

SHORT-DISTANCE HYPERDRIVE POD

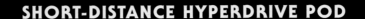

HYPERDRIVE-EQUIPPED INFILTRATION PODS are designed to deliver a droid to a specific destination. This means that they are often used for spying and assassination missions. These pods are outfitted with only the barest essentials, so they are not suitable for living beings.

DATA FILE

TYPE: Pod ship
MANUFACTURER: Arakyd Industries
SPEED: 750 kph (466 mph)
MODEL: X3-13
LENGTH: 11.7 m (38 ft 4 in)
HYPERDRIVE: Class 0.5
WEAPONS: None

Landing thrusters

SEEKING POD

Infiltration pods are equipped with a long-range communications system, while their hyperdrive allows for short-range searches. Landing thrusters assist for a quiet approach.

Hyperdrive

Long-range transmitter

Wide Search

In its search for the rebels, the Empire sends out hundreds of pods loaded with Imperial probe droids. They are programmed to search for any rebel installations.

The rebel crew of the *Ghost* find themselves hunted by a deadly infiltrator droid piloting a tactical infiltration pod. They barely manage to blast it out of the sky!

NABOO STARFIGHTER

N-1 STARFIGHTER

BOLD AND BEAUTIFUL in its design, the N-1 starfighter is the signature ship of the Royal Naboo Security Forces. Its forward section is clad in chromium for ceremonial display, and its sleek shape is as much an expression of art as of aerodynamics.

YELLOW TAILS
The Naboo starfighter's long tail acts as a power charge collector. The similarly shaped engine tails serve as heat sinks.

High-voltage charging tail

Cockpit

Astromech droid port

Royal chromium finish

Torpedo tube

Autopilot Anakin
In the Battle of Naboo, young Anakin Skywalker accidentally launches an N-1 starfighter. It ends up destroying the Trade Federation's battle droid control ship.

N-1 starfighters fly over Naboo during the celebrations to mark the end of the Empire.

VULTURE DROID

VULTURE-CLASS STARFIGHTER

DATA FILE

TYPE: Droid starfighter
MANUFACTURER: Xi Charrian
SPEED: 1,180 kph (733 mph)
MODEL: *Vulture*-class
LENGTH: 3.5 m (11 ft 6 in)
HYPERDRIVE: None
WEAPONS: Twin blaster cannons, 2 energy torpedo launchers, buzz droid launchers

THESE MERCILESS DROID STARFIGHTERS are controlled by a central computer, and carry no living pilot. They originate with the Trade Federation, but the Separatist Alliance puts these deadly, convertible vehicles into service during the Clone Wars. Their only weak point for enemy fire is their anti-gravity generators.

Droid brain located above sensor ports

Energy torpedo launcher

Flight mode claw

Scissor-like walking action

Automated Droid Deployment Stations are capable of launching six vulture droids at once.

ALL CHANGE

The vulture droid can swiftly change from a starfighter to a walker for land battles. A "head" unit extends for improved sensor readings. The "legs" of the ship are built with powerful shock absorbers.

Self-Preservation

Squadrons of vulture droids race to defend the Trade Federation's Droid Control Ship orbiting Naboo from N-1 starfighters.

HYENA BOMBER

HYENA-CLASS BOMBER

DROID BRAINS CONTROL THESE deadly ships, which are deployed by the Separatists during the Clone Wars. They are designed to carry out precision-targeted bombing raids from the air, before transforming into walker mode and wreaking further havoc on the ground.

The hyena bomber's design is based on that of the vulture droids. However, they have wider and sturdier hulls as well as bigger wings.

Photoreceptor "eyes"

Ordnance pod

Wings become legs in walker mode

Up in Flames
Hyena bombers wipe out Twi'lek villages on the planet Ryloth, but are destroyed by Anakin Skywalker and Ahsoka Tano before they can reach the capital city, Lessu.

ADVANCED ATTACKER
The *Hyena*-class droid bomber has two hull units. Its starboard unit contains the droid's central processor unit, while the secondary port unit contains the droid's ordnance bay, which drops bombs with lethal accuracy.

GEONOSIAN STARFIGHTER

TERRITORIAL DEFENSE STARFIGHTER

DATA FILE

TYPE: Starfighter
MANUFACTURER: Huppla Pasa Tisc Shipwrights Collective
SPEED: 1,250 kph (776 mph)
MODEL: *Nantex*-class territorial defense starfighter
LENGTH: 9.8 m (32 ft 1 in)
HYPERDRIVE: None
WEAPONS: 1 laser cannon turret

THESE FAST FIGHTERS may be unshielded, but they defend the Geonosian population well. They swarm furiously over any and all opposition. These vessels are rarely seen beyond the Geonosian homeworld, because they are difficult ships for non-Geonosians to master.

The Separatist forces reveal the full might of these unusual starfighters during the First Battle of Geonosis.

One-pilot cockpit with 360° views

Small, powerful engine

Needle-nosed design

Laser cannon with wide range of movement

Storm of Ships

The Republic encounters these vicious fighters again during the second Battle of Geonosis. Republic forces struggle desperately to drop LAATs into position at Point Rain.

NOT EASY

The Geonosian starfighter is a complicated ship. It is equipped with a unique engine system, which is difficult to read on sensors. It also uses a complex multi-axis control system.

FANBLADE FIGHTER

GINIVEX-CLASS FANBLADE STARFIGHTER

DATA FILE

TYPE: Starfighter
MANUFACTURER:
Huppla Pasa Tisc
Shipwrights Collective
SPEED: 1,250 kph (777 mph)
MODEL: *Ginivex*-class
starfighter
LENGTH: 13.1 m (42 ft 11 in)
HYPERDRIVE: Class 1
WEAPONS: 2 laser cannons

JUST SIX SHIPS were built to this design for Sith apprentice Asajj Ventress. The large sail makes the fanblade an extremely fast ship and gives it greater shield strength. However, the shield's energy output makes it easy for other ships' sensors to detect.

Cockpit

FOLDING FAN

The fanblade fighter's sail can be retracted for landing or in flight, and a backup sail can also be deployed in its place. When the sail is retracted, the laser cannons at its tips rotate to remain facing forward.

Retractable
solar sail

Laser
cannon

Asajj Attacks

Ventress uses one of her fanblades to attack Anakin Skywalker's *Venator*-class Star Destroyer, the *Resolute*.

93

After Ventress crashes a fanblade fighter into the hangar of her own flagship, she faces Jedi Knights Obi-Wan Kenobi and Anakin Skywalker in lightsaber combat.

SOULLESS ONE

BELBULLAB-22 STARFIGHTER

GENERAL GRIEVOUS'S personal ship is a modified Belbullab-22 starfighter. Despite its impressive armaments, the cyborg general tends to use the agile craft for escaping from danger rather than as a Separatist fighter.

DATA FILE

TYPE: Starfighter
MANUFACTURER: Feethan Ottraw Scalable Assemblies
SPEED: 1,100 kph (684 mph)
MODEL: Belbullab-22
LENGTH: 6.7 m (21 ft 11 in)
HYPERDRIVE: Class 2
WEAPONS: Triple rapid-fire laser cannons

ALL IN ONE
Soulless One has long-range scanners built in at the front and a well-armored shield generator directly behind the cockpit.

Cockpit

Triple laser cannon

Resilient impervium hull

Soulless Asylum
When Order 66 causes the Republic's clone troopers to turn against their Jedi generals, Obi-Wan Kenobi steals Grievous's ship and uses it to escape his former allies.

During the Battle of Bothawui, General Grievous abandons his frigate and flees in his Belbullab-22 starfighter.

TRI-FIGHTER

DROID FIGHTER

DATA FILE

TYPE: Droid starfighter
MANUFACTURER: Phlac-Arphocc Automata Industries
SPEED: 1,050 kph (652 mph)
MODEL: Tri-fighter
LENGTH: 5.4 m (17 ft 4 in)
HYPERDRIVE: None
WEAPONS: 4 light laser cannons, buzz-droid deployment missiles

Tilt-and-slide laser cannon

Pair of red, eye-like optical sensors

Fixed-position laser cannon

THE DROID TRI-FIGHTER does not require a pilot. Instead, the ship itself is the body of the droid, whose sole purpose is to destroy enemy craft. The Separatist forces start using tri-fighters toward the end of the Clone Wars.

BAD DROID

The tri-fighter's advanced droid brain is programmed for aggressive behavior. Its buzz-droid missiles can reduce a ship to scrap in seconds!

Main reactor core in rotating frame

Starfighter Swarm

Tri-fighters swarm toward Anakin Skywalker and Obi-Wan Kenobi during the Battle of Coruscant. As they do so, they destroy everything in their path.

Tri-fighters fly in large groups during Clone Wars battles. Their numbers make up for their relatively small size!

DELTA-7 LIGHT INTERCEPTOR

SPECIALIZED JEDI STARFIGHTER

DATA FILE

TYPE: Starfighter
MANUFACTURER: Kuat Systems Engineering
SPEED: 1,260 kph (783 mph)
MODEL: Delta-7 *Aethersprite*-class light interceptor
LENGTH: 8 m (26 ft 3 in)
HYPERDRIVE: Class 1 with external hyperdrive ring
WEAPONS: Dual rapid-fire laser cannons

THE DELTA-7 IS DESIGNED specifically for the Jedi and is in frequent use long before the Clone Wars begin. As more Jedi leave the temples to join the war effort, their combat ships are swiftly upgraded to keep pace with the enemy's crafts. This prompts the creation of the Delta-7B.

Astromech droid

Laser cannon

DELTA MAKEOVER

There are small improvements from the Delta-7 to the 7B. The Delta-7 has a wing port for an astromech, while the 7B places the port in front of the cockpit. The Delta-7B also boasts a tougher central hull than its predecessor.

Evasive Action

While engaging in a dogfight with Jango and Boba Fett over Geonosis, Obi-Wan Kenobi fakes his own death when he realizes his Delta-7 is no match for the superior *Slave I*.

The Delta-7 does not have a built-in hyperdrive. It must be attached to an external hyperspace transport ring.

ETA-2 LIGHT INTERCEPTOR

JEDI STARFIGHTER

DATA FILE

TYPE: Starfighter
MANUFACTURER: Kuat Systems Engineering
SPEED: 1,500 kph (932 mph)
MODEL: Eta-2 *Actis*-class light interceptor
LENGTH: 5.4 m (17 ft 8 in)
HYPERDRIVE: Class 1 with external hyperdrive ring
WEAPONS: 2 forward-mounted laser cannons, 2 rear-mounted laser cannons, proton torpedoes

THE ETA-2 INTERCEPTOR'S POPULARITY with the Jedi Order earns it the nickname the Jedi Starfighter. It is one of the fastest and most responsive starships produced during the Clone Wars. Almost every Jedi flies one, customizing the craft to meet their unique skills and requirements.

Spacious cockpit

Twin ion engine

Proton torpedo

MAKING CHOICES
The Jedi starfighter uses heavy weaponry, but the power drain prevents constant firing. Most Jedi remove the sensors and targeting equipment to save weight and space.

The fast Jedi Interceptor has a thin hull made of moveable segments. This weakness is easily exploited by Separatist buzz droids.

Rescue Mission
Obi-Wan Kenobi and Anakin Skywalker fly Jedi starfighters into battle over Coruscant in an effort to save Chancellor Palpatine from Count Dooku.

V-19 TORRENT STARFIGHTER

TRI-FOIL FIGHTER CRAFT

DATA FILE

TYPE: Starfighter
MANUFACTURER: Slayn & Korpil
SPEED: 1,200 kph (745 mph)
MODEL: V-19 Torrent starfighter
LENGTH: 6 m (19 ft 8 in)
HYPERDRIVE: Class 1 (early models use external hyperdrive ring)
WEAPONS: 2 laser cannons, concussion missiles

THE V-19 IS USED during the early days of the Clone Wars. It becomes a popular fighter for the rapidly expanding Republic Navy. Originally designed to be a short-range fighter, the V-19 later undergoes a series of upgrades that make it suitable for much longer flights.

WEAPONS

Each wingtip of the V-19 has a mounted laser cannon, and dual folding S-foils give it exceptional maneuverability. It also stocks six powerful concussion missiles.

Sliding cockpit

Folding S-foil

Ventral airfoil

Laser cannon

Ahsoka Tano leads a squad of V-19s into battle to try and break a Separatist blockade over Ryloth. The V-19s perform well, but only two of the squad survive, and the mission is lost.

Staying Close

During Republic missions, the V-19s are often deployed from large Republic attack cruisers. They return to them when the mission is over.

V-WING

ALPHA-3 *NIMBUS*-CLASS V-WING STARFIGHTER

DATA FILE

TYPE: Starfighter
MANUFACTURER: Kuat Systems Engineering
SPEED: 1,450 kph (901 mph)
MODEL: Alpha-3 *Nimbus*
LENGTH: 7.9 m (25 ft 11 in)
HYPERDRIVE: None
WEAPONS: 2 twin rapid-fire laser cannons

SMALL, FAST, AND AGILE, the V-wing starfighter is used late in the Clone Wars by the Republic. With little in the way of firepower or armor, V-wing pilots use swarm strategies to overwhelm their opponents, assisted by an astromech droid.

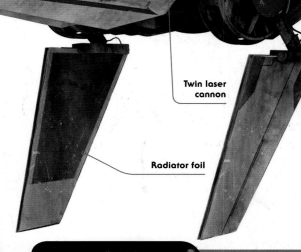

Deflector shield heat sink

Astromech droid

Twin laser cannon

Radiator foil

EMPEROR'S REIGN

V-wings are used by the Imperial Navy during the early years of the Empire. Darth Vader, in an Eta-2 *Actis*-class light interceptor, leads a squadron of V-wings to hunt down an Imperial ship that has been hijacked by Twi'lek rebels.

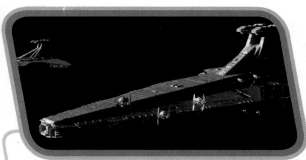

Starfighter Swarm

V-wings do not have hyperdrives, so the ships are most often deployed in large quantities from hyperdrive-enabled *Venator*-class star destroyers.

After making himself Emperor, Palpatine takes his shuttle to the planet Coruscant with an escort of V-wing fighters.

ARC-170 STARFIGHTER

AGGRESSIVE RECONNAISSANCE FIGHTER

DATA FILE

TYPE: Starfighter
MANUFACTURERS: Incom
Corporation with
Subpro Corporation
SPEED: 1,050 kph (652 mph)
MODEL: ARC-170
LENGTH: 14.5 m (47 ft 7 in)
HYPERDRIVE: Class 1.5
WEAPONS: 2 forward-
mounted laser cannons,
2 rear-mounted laser
cannons, proton
torpedoes

THIS THREE-PERSON STARFIGHTER is durable and reliable. It carries a formidable arsenal, as well as sufficient supplies for five days. It should come as no surprise that the ARC-170s rapidly replace the V-19s as the Republic's primary dogfighter during the Clone Wars.

X-WING TEMPLATE

The ARC-170s are so dependable that both Empire and rebel forces continue to use the starfighters after the Clone Wars. They become the template for the first generation of X-wings.

Astromech droid

Paired engine

Clone troopers serving Jedi Plo Koon are flying ARC-170s when Palpatine issues Order 66, commanding the troopers to take Koon's life.

Battle Protection

During the Battle of Coruscant, a squadron of ARC-170s protects Anakin Skywalker and Obi-Wan Kenobi on their mission to rescue Chancellor Palpatine.

Laser cannon

UMBARAN STARFIGHTER

UNIQUE FIGHTER CRAFT

Clone troopers Fives and Hardcase steal a pair of Umbaran starfighters and use them to sneak onto a Separatist ship.

DATA FILE

TYPE: Starfighter
MANUFACTURER: Ghost Armaments
SPEED: 1,100 kph (684 mph)
MODEL: Zenuas 33
LENGTH: 10.4 m (34 ft 2 in)
HYPERDRIVE: None
WEAPONS: 2 wing-mounted missile pods, plasma cannon

THESE VESSELS ARE some of the most advanced starfighters in the galaxy. The pilot sits inside a ray-shield cockpit and steers using touch-sensitive holograms. Non-Umbarans find learning to fly them difficult.

Ray-shield cockpit

Stabilizer fin

IN A SPIN

Umbaran starfighters are far more agile than most ships. They can rotate on the spot with no need to bank or circle, so are able to change direction and target enemies instantly.

Flexible wings

Plasma cannon

Missile pod

Light in the Dark

Republic forces fare badly against Umbaran starfighters during the Battle of Umbara. The native species and its ships are well adapted for life on a world where it is always night.

GAUNTLET STARFIGHTER

KOM'RK-CLASS FIGHTER

KOM'RK-CLASS FIGHTERS ARE flown by the Death Watch—a Mandalorian splinter group that seeks a return to its planet's warrior past. These fast ships serve as both fighters and troop transports. Up to 24 soldiers can travel aboard, deploying from the rear of the ship using jetpacks.

Darth Maul acquires his own *Kom'rk*-class ship when he briefly seizes control of Mandalore.

Cockpit

Turbojet

Laser cannon

Rotating wings

SMALLER SHIP

A second version of the *Kom'rk*-class fighter measures just 52.3 m (171 ft 7 in) long. The ship's laser cannons are recessed in the center of its nose.

Run the Gauntlet

The Gauntlet starfighters are hidden on Mandalore's moon Concordia. Obi-Wan Kenobi and Satine Kryze discover them while trying to escape the Death Watch.

FANG FIGHTER

MANDALORIAN STARFIGHTER

DATA FILE

TYPE: Starfighter
MANUFACTURER:
MandalMotors
SPEED: 900 kph (559 mph)
MODEL: *Fang*-class
LENGTH: 6 m (19 ft 8 in)
HYPERDRIVE: Class 2
WEAPONS: 2 wing-mounted
laser cannons, proton
torpedo launcher

ALSO KNOWN AS THE
Protectorate fighter, this
fast ship features wings
that swivel around the
cockpit. This presents an
ever-changing target for
attackers and provides
vectored thrust control for
an almost unparalleled
level of maneuverability.

Mandalorian Protectors in
Fang fighters attack Hera
Syndulla and Sabine Wren
when they approach the
planet Concord Dawn.

Ion engine

Laser
cannon

Stable fuselage

Pivoting wing

Mandalorian
Protectors symbol

Fang Fightback

Imperial Star Destroyers attack
the rebel base on the planet
Atollon. Sabine Wren and
a group of Mandalorian
Protectors in Fang fighters
mount a spirited defense.

IN A SPIN

The Fang fighter's
laser cannons fire
an arcing assault
as its wings rotate.
Its proton torpedo
launcher is hidden,
causing opponents
to underestimate
its firepower.

XANADU BLOOD

BOUNTY HUNTER STARFIGHTER

DATA FILE

TYPE: Starfighter
MANUFACTURER: Baktoid Workshop
SPEED: 1,200 kph (745 mph)
MODEL: *Rogue*-class
LENGTH: 12.7 m (41 ft 8 in)
HYPERDRIVE: Class 2
WEAPONS: 2 laser cannons

THE *XANADU BLOOD* IS a heavily modified *Rogue*-class starfighter. The Separatists give it to the notorious bounty hunter Cad Bane as payment for services to Darth Sidious. The ship is equipped with an expensive and rare cloaking device, allowing Bane to strike his enemies unseen.

High-power laser cannon

Powerful port thruster

CHANGES
Several changes have been made to the *Xanadu Blood*. The modified cabin allows room for three passengers, and the engine has been altered to run silently for brief periods.

Cad Bane uses his ship to hunt down Force-sensitive children and deliver them to Mustafar for Darth Sidious.

Cockpit

Forward scanners

Follow the Trail
Anakin is able to gain access to the *Xanadu Blood*'s fueling log. This shows him which planets Cad Bane has flown the ship to.

TIE FIGHTER

TWIN ION ENGINE STARFIGHTER

DATA FILE

TYPE: Starfighter
MANUFACTURER: Sienar
Fleet Systems
SPEED: 1,200 kph (746 mph)
MODEL: Twin Ion Engine
line edition space
superiority starfighter
LENGTH: 7.2 m (23 ft 9 in)
HYPERDRIVE: None
WEAPONS: 2 L-s1 laser
cannons

THE ROAR OF A TIE FIGHTER engine inspires fear throughout the Empire. Produced in vast numbers, these short-range combat craft police the skies of Imperial worlds and defend capital spaceships in fast-moving squadrons. Their twin ion engines are fast and light, and are powered by solar collectors.

NO FRILLS
Unlike most other combat ships, the TIE fighter is not equipped with shields. It has life-support features, but pilots also wear flight suits to breathe and guard against decompression.

Solar collector

The Swarm
The preferred strategy of TIE squadrons is to swarm enemies with a mass of ships, overwhelming the opposition with numbers rather than firepower.

Viewport

Laser cannon

Ezra Bridger and Zeb Orrelios steal a TIE fighter. Their fellow rebel Sabine Wren decides to give it a colorful paint job in her familiar street-art style.

TIE BOMBER

TWIN ION ENGINE BOMBER

DATA FILE

TYPE: Bomber
MANUFACTURER:
Sienar Fleet Systems
SPEED: 850 kph (528 mph)
MODEL: Twin Ion Engine
surface assault bomber
LENGTH: 9.2 m (30 ft 2 in)
HYPERDRIVE: None
WEAPONS: 2 laser
cannons, concussion
missiles, orbital mines,
proton bombs

BIGGER AND LESS maneuverable than a standard TIE fighter, this bomber is built for surface assaults rather than fighter-to-fighter combat. Its secondary hull is entirely given over to mission-specific weaponry, which can be targeted with pinpoint precision.

TIE bombers are launched from an Imperial cruiser above the planet Ryloth for a strike on Cham Syndulla's rebel cell.

Ordnance pod

Missile port

Wing pylon

Targeting sensors

Solar collectors

BREATHE EASY

The TIE bomber has its own built-in life-support system. However, TIE bomber pilots still wear flight suits with breathing gear, in case of an emergency.

Asteroid Attack

The Empire uses TIE bombers to bombard an asteroid field near the Hoth system in an effort to flush out rebel ship the *Millennium Falcon*.

TIE INTERCEPTOR

TWIN ION ENGINE INTERCEPTOR

DATA FILE

TYPE: Starfighter
MANUFACTURER: Sienar
Fleet Systems
SPEED: 1,250 kph (777 mph)
MODEL: Twin Ion Engine
interceptor
LENGTH: 9.6 m (31 ft 6 in)
HYPERDRIVE: None
WEAPONS: 4 laser cannons

FASTER AND MORE AGILE
than the standard TIE fighter,
the interceptor is introduced
as a response to the growing
rebel threat. Its main function
is to destroy rebel starfighters,
which it achieves with rarely
matched accuracy. It eventually
makes up one fifth of the
Imperial Navy's starfighter fleet!

The Empire has TIE
interceptors patrolling
the area around the
partially constructed
second Death Star.

Cockpit

Targeting sensor

Solar collector

Laser
cannon

ACE PILOTS ONLY

TIE interceptors are flown by the most
experienced Imperial pilots. They use an
advanced targeting system superior to
that of the standard TIE fighter. It is linked
to the vessel's wingtip laser cannons.

Second Place

An *Arquitens*-class command
cruiser deploys several TIE
interceptors to attack a rebel
transport ship carrying supplies.

TIE ADVANCED V1

DATA FILE

TYPE: Starfighter
MANUFACTURER: Sienar Fleet Systems
SPEED: 1,600 kph (994 mph)
MODEL: Twin Ion Engine Advanced v1
LENGTH: 3.6 m (11 ft 9 in)
HYPERDRIVE: Class 4.5
WEAPONS: 2 laser cannons, missile launcher

THE FIRST TIE ADVANCED V1 is unveiled on Lothal during Empire Day—and is immediately destroyed by rebels! These unusual ships are mainly used by Force-sensitive Imperial agents known as Inquisitors. These fierce Jedi-hunters fly their v1s across the galaxy on their missions to find—and stop—anyone who uses the Force.

SO MUCH FOR SOLAR

The v1 is the only TIE fighter to have armor instead of solar collectors on the outside of its wings. This means it can only use solar power for its less energy-intensive systems.

Armored outer S-foil "wing"

Shots Fired

Chopper hijacks a v1 that belongs to an Inquisitor known only as the Eighth Brother. He uses it to attack a former Sith—Lord Maul!

Transparisteel cockpit

Laser cannon

The Fifth Brother and the Seventh Sister use v1s during their mission to kidnap Force-sensitive children.

Solar collector

TIE ADVANCED X1

VADER'S STARFIGHTER

DATA FILE

TYPE: Starfighter
MANUFACTURER: Sienar Fleet Systems
SPEED: 1,200 kph (746 mph)
MODEL: Twin Ion Engine Advanced x1
LENGTH: 9.2 m (30 ft 2 in)
HYPERDRIVE: Class 4
WEAPONS: 2 laser cannons

DARTH VADER FLIES AN early prototype of the TIE Advanced x1, with a custom cockpit for his unique armor. Unlike standard TIE fighters, it has a deflector shield and a hyperdrive. Its low profile is made possible by the high-specification solar collectors on its wings.

Darth Vader's compact TIE Advanced x1 is flanked by two standard TIE fighters in the Battle of Yavin.

High-spec solar cells

Entry/exit hatch

Laser cannon

Maintenance access bay

Expert Pilot

Darth Vader is one of the best pilots in the galaxy, which is why he is the best person to test out the Empire's latest starfighters in battle.

DARK SPEED

The Advanced x1 is as much Darth Vader's personal shuttle as it is his favored fighter. It is a rare example of a TIE craft that can travel faster than light.

TIE DEFENDER

TWIN ION ENGINE DEFENDER

THIS EXPERIMENTAL STARFIGHTER never completed its prototype stage. It is used in limited numbers only against a small rebel cell led by Hera Syndulla, but still poses a serious threat. The TIE defender is the first TIE to have a hyperdrive and deflector shields, and it can travel incredibly fast in real space.

DATA FILE

TYPE: Starfighter
MANUFACTURER: Sienar Fleet Systems
SPEED: 1,680 kph (1,045 mph)
MODEL: Twin Ion Engine/D Defender
LENGTH: 9.2 m (30 ft 2 in)
HYPERDRIVE: Class 2
WEAPONS: 6 laser cannons, concussion missiles, proton torpedoes

POWER OF THREE

The TIE defender's three solar-collector wings allow for increased energy use and are each equipped with computer-controlled maneuvering jets.

Sensor array

Missile launcher

Laser cannon

Solar collector

Fireproof Fighter

When TIE defenders are sent to capture the rebel Senator Mon Mothma, they follow the rebel ship the *Ghost* into the Archeon Nebula. There, the experimental ships prove capable of surviving the extreme heat given off by a newly forming star.

Grand Admiral Thrawn of the Imperial Navy pushes for the TIE defender's development.

MINING GUILD TIE FIGHTER

MODIFIED SPACE SUPERIORITY STARFIGHTER

Mining Guild insignia

DATA FILE

TYPE: Starfighter
MANUFACTURER: Sienar
Fleet Systems
SPEED: 950 kph (590 mph)
MODEL: Modified
TIE/ln starfighter
LENGTH: 7.2 m (23 ft 7 in)
HYPERDRIVE: None
WEAPONS: 2 L-s1
laser cannons

THESE BRIGHTLY COLORED TIE fighters represent part of a deal between the Empire and the Mining Guild. In exchange for valuable resources, the Empire supplies the Guild with modified ships.

THE SAME BUT DIFFERENT

Where Imperial TIEs have six solar collectors on each wing, the Mining Guild version has just four, making it less powerful. To further help with identification, Mining Guild fighters are painted yellow.

Mine Craft

When Ezra Bridger comes under attack from Mining Guild TIE fighters, he slices off one of their wings with his lightsaber. Impressively, he does this while riding on a space creature called a purrgil!

Solar collectors

Pressurized cockpit

The rebel crew of the *Ghost* encounter Mining Guild TIE fighters when they set out to raid a gas mining installation.

A-WING

RZ-1 A-WING INTERCEPTER

DATA FILE

TYPE: Starfighter
MANUFACTURER: Kuat Systems Engineering
SPEED: 1,300 kph (808 mph)
MODEL: RZ-1 A-wing
LENGTH: 9.6 m (31 ft 6 in)
HYPERDRIVE: Class 1
WEAPONS: 2 laser cannons, missile launchers

THE A-WING IS ONE of the fastest fighters on either side in the Galactic Civil War. With a design influenced by Republic starfighters, A-wings are protected by powerful deflector shields and armor. However, as the Rebellion progresses they are stripped of their defenses and heavy weapons in order to make them even faster.

Stabilizer wing

Cockpit

Laser cannon

PHOENIX FLYER

The A-wing is the main fighter used by the rebel cell called Phoenix Squadron. The ships are useful for intelligence operations as well as combat, because each one contains a datalog that can be ejected if the vessel is intercepted.

Missile tube

End over Endor

Green Leader Arvel Crynyd flies his A-wing into the bridge of the Super Star Destroyer *Executor* during the Battle of Endor, destroying the mighty warship.

Ezra Bridger flies an A-wing trainer ship belonging to Phoenix Squadron. The RZ-1T is modified to include an instructor's seat.

BLADE WING

PROTOTYPE B-WING STARFIGHTER

DATA FILE

TYPE: Starfighter
MANUFACTURER: Quarrie
SPEED: 950 kph (590 mph)
MODEL: Prototype B-wing
LENGTH: 16.9 m (55 ft 5 in)
HYPERDRIVE: Non-functional
WEAPONS: 3 ion cannons, 2 high intensity blasters, 1 prototype composite beam laser, proton torpedoes

THE BLADE WING IS designed by a Mon Calamari ship builder named Quarrie. This prototype combines unusual key features from several ships from the Clone Wars (most notably the V-19 starfighter and the T-6 shuttle). The end result is versatile and powerful, but expensive and difficult to maintain.

Gyroscopic cockpit

Gunner's turret

Shield generator and hyperdrive housing

Ion cannon mounted on S-foil

PROS AND CONS

The Blade Wing includes a secondary gunner station, and the cockpit design allows the pilot to remain level with the horizon. Unfortunately, when the composite beam system is fired, it drains the hyperdrive.

One in a Million

Hera uses a single blast from the Blade Wing to take out a massive Imperial blockade ship. Her success makes the rebels realize that they need to develop this prototype into a starfighter model in their fight against the Empire.

Quarrie will not let the rebels use the Blade Wing in battle until Hera Syndulla proves that she can fly it.

B-WING

HEAVY WEAPONS FIGHTER

DATA FILE

TYPE: Starfighter
MANUFACTURER: Slayn & Korpil
SPEED: 950 kph (590 mph)
MODEL: A/SF-01 B-wing
LENGTH: 16.9 m (55 ft 5 in)
HYPERDRIVE: Class 2
WEAPONS: 4 laser cannons, proton torpedoes, ion cannon

Gyroscopic command pod

THE B-WING DEFIES conventional starfighter design by adopting gyroscopic mechanics. It enables the bulk of the ship to rotate rapidly around the side-cockpit, which remains level. This approach, combined with the ion cannon, makes the B-wing an ideal choice when battling larger ships.

Deployed S-foil

COSTLY CRAFT

An advanced targeting computer allows all B-wings to operate on a single network. Due to cost and maintenance issues, the ships are eventually retired, with many of their parts later repurposed into Resistance troop transports.

Wingtip ion cannon

Heavy weapons pod

A ship designer named Quarrie develops the prototype B-wing. He only shares it with the rebels after Hera Syndulla proves she is capable of flying the ship.

Warfare Roles

The B-wing takes part in the Battle of Endor. However, due to its poor performance in dogfights, it is initially held back for use against the larger capital ships, while the X-wings engage the TIE fighters.

U-WING

REBEL GUNSHIP

THE U-WING IS A UNIQUE swing-wing starship that handles like a repulsorcraft. U-wings are designed for close surface flight, and delivering troops to battle. They are invaluable to the rebel fleet during the Battle of Scarif. Sadly, few of them escape the planet's atmosphere after the Death Star attacks.

DATA FILE

TYPE: Gunship
MANUFACTURER: Incom Corporation
SPEED: 950 kph (590 mph)
MODEL: UT-60 U-wing starfighter/transport
LENGTH: 25 m (82 ft)
HYPERDRIVE: Class 1
WEAPONS: 2 laser cannons, 1 repeating ion blaster

U-wings make up part of the rebel Blue Squadron. They swoop into action during the Battle of Scarif.

FUEL GUZZLER

A major advantage of the U-wing is that its floor can be customized to hold different guns. However, it has a big drawback: its hyperdrive consumes large quantities of fuel.

Fusion chamber

Sloping cockpit window

Fusial thrust engine

Front intake

Swing-wing S-foils

Rogue Missions

Jyn Erso, Cassian Andor, and K-2SO use a U-wing to travel to Jedha. From there, they fly with Bodhi Rook to the planet Eadu, where they crash and are forced to abandon ship.

Forward, non-attack wing formation

T-65 X-WING

FOUR-WINGED REBEL ATTACK SHIPS

X-WINGS ARE DESIGNED TO excel in all areas of starfighter combat, and have no discernable weaknesses. These sturdy ships become the centerpiece of several crucial battles, and their unmistakable appearance makes them a symbol of the heroic Rebel Alliance.

DATA FILE

TYPE: Starfighter
MANUFACTURER: Incom Corporation
SPEED: 1,050 kph (652 mph)
MODEL: T-65B X-wing
LENGTH: 13.4 m (44 ft)
HYPERDRIVE: Class 1
WEAPONS: 4 laser cannons, proton torpedo launcher

Yavin Hero

At the Battle of Yavin, Luke Skywalker scores a famous victory when he opts to rely on the Force instead of his X-wing's advanced targeting systems.

Astromech

Folding S-foils

TOUGH AND NIMBLE

The X-wing is designed for assault runs on larger ships, such as Imperial Star Destroyers. It is highly maneuverable and heavily shielded. Each craft also has an astromech docking port for navigational assistance, and is stocked with emergency supplies to last up to one week.

Laser cannon

Wedge Antilles pilots an X-wing through the heart of the second Death Star, with devastating results.

Y-WING

BTL-A4 Y-WING ASSAULT STARFIGHTER

DATA FILE

TYPE: Starfighter/bomber
MANUFACTURER:
Koensayr Manufacturing
SPEED: 1,000 kph (621 mph)
MODEL: BTL-A4 Y-wing
LENGTH: 16 m (52 ft 6 in)
HYPERDRIVE: Class 1
WEAPONS: 2 laser
cannons, 2 proton
torpedo launchers, 1 twin
ion cannon, proton bombs

DESIGNED FOR BOMBING RAIDS, the Y-wing is a sleek ship originally used by the Galactic Republic. Y-wings find new life as starfighters for the Rebel Alliance during the Galactic Civil War. Stripped of every non-essential system and endlessly repaired by rebel mechanics, they remain popular with Alliance pilots.

Vectral ring

Sensor dome

The first Y-wings used in the Clone Wars have a gunner's station above the cockpit. In later models, one operator serves as pilot and gunner.

Twin ion cannon

Laser cannon

Astromech droid

Transparisteel cockpit canopy

Gold Stars

The Y-wing pilots of Gold Squadron form an important part of the rebel strike force that takes on the Empire's first Death Star.

BARE BONES

The exposed mechanics of the Y-wing's hull and engine nacelle plating make it easier for the Rebel Alliance to maintain and repair the aging craft.

SPECIAL FORCES TIE FIGHTER

TIE/SF SPACE SUPERIORITY FIGHTER

THIS ADVANCED TIE FIGHTER is used as both a combat vehicle and a patrol ship. Its familiar design echoes the earlier model of the sinister regime that pioneered it—the Empire. However, it does improve and adapt many of the technological shortcomings of the original design, making it a much more powerful starfighter!

Communications antenna

Spherical, two-seater cockpit

Solar power converter

Transparisteel front viewport

Solar array wing

HIGH TECH

The TIE/sf starfighter is equipped with deflector shields and an advanced flight computer. It also has a hyperdrive, unlike regular First Order TIE fighters.

Tricky Escape

Finn and Poe Dameron steal a TIE/sf during their escape from the First Order. They don't realize that it is still attached to a cable—until they try to take off!

Only the elite pilots of the First Order Special Forces may use the TIE/sf fighters. They take part in the Battle of Takodana and engage Resistance X-wings.

TIE SILENCER

TIE/VN PROTOTYPE

DATA FILE

TYPE: Starfighter
MANUFACTURER: Sienar-Jaemus Fleet Systems
MODEL: TIE/vn prototype
LENGTH: 17.43 m (57 ft 2 in)
HYPERDRIVE: Equipped
WEAPONS: 2 heavy laser cannons, 2 medium laser cannons, 2 proton torpedo launchers

THE TIE SILENCER IS an advanced TIE fighter prototype built specially for Kylo Ren. One of the most powerful starfighters in the First Order fleet, its heavy weapons can crack even the thick armor of massive cruisers. Although it is large for a one-pilot ship, the silencer is both fast and agile.

Dark Side Ace

Incredible piloting skills run in Kylo's family, and his Force abilities make him a lethal adversary in space combat. Unfortunately the Resistance only discovers this when it is too late.

Armored cockpit canopy

Heavy laser cannon

Advanced solar collector panel

Torpedo launcher

Kylo prepares to launch a volley of torpedoes at the *Raddus*' bridge, but his wingmate fires first. The explosion wipes out many Resistance officers.

HIGH-TECH TERROR

The silencer features many advanced pieces of technology that make it even more deadly: heavy laser cannons, tough deflector shields, unique torpedo launchers, and a stealth field generator that hides it from enemy sensors.

T-70 X-WING

RESISTANCE STARFIGHTER

AFTER DEFEATING THE Empire, the New Republic adopts the famous rebel X-wings as official defenders of the government. Using official resources and technological advances, the new generation of X-wings is faster and more heavily armored.

The best pilot in the Resistance, Poe Dameron, has his own T-70 X-wing codenamed *Black One*.

KX12 laser cannons

Incom-FreiTek 5L5 fusial thrust engines

Battle-damaged nose wedge

BB-8 in astromech droid loading area

UNBEATABLE

The T-70 is capable of both space and atmospheric combat, and is virtually unmatched in close-quarters dogfights. It includes an undercarriage-mounted blaster cannon, which is controlled by an automated computer targeting system.

Frontline Attack

The T-70 X-wings become part of General Leia Organa's Resistance against the First Order.

RESISTANCE BOMBER

MG-100 STARFORTRESS

THIS UNUSUAL LOOKING SHIP carries a devastating payload: hundreds of powerful proton bombs. The MG-100 also bristles with laser cannons, allowing it to battle its way to its target and then rain destruction. Even the largest First Order ships fear the StarFortress!

DATA FILE

TYPE: Heavy bomber
MANUFACTURER: Slayn & Korpil
MODEL: MG-100 StarFortress SF-17
LENGTH: 29.67 m (97 ft 4 in)
HYPERDRIVE: Equipped
WEAPONS: 3 laser cannon turrets, 6 medium laser cannons, proton bombs

Short-range comms antenna

Armored flight deck

Rear turret

Sublight engine

The StarFortress has a crew of five, including two specialist gunners. The gunners defend the ship, firing at the enemy from exposed turrets in the ship's rear and underside.

BIG BANG

The StarFortress' strange shape comes from the large, detachable bomb bay that slots into the bottom of the ship's hull.

Bomb bay

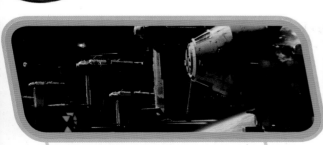

Bombing Run

High above D'Qar, the StarFortresses of Cobalt and Crimson squadrons attack the mighty Star Destroyers of the First Order fleet.

Targeting sensor

H-TYPE NUBIAN YACHT

SHIMMERING SENATOR'S SHIP

DATA FILE

TYPE: Yacht
MANUFACTURER: Theed Palace Space Vessel Engineering Corps
SPEED: 8,000 kph (4,971 mph)
MODEL: H-type
LENGTH: 47.9 m (157 ft 2 in)
HYPERDRIVE: Class 0.9
WEAPONS: None

THIS YACHT IS THE personal transport of Senator Padmé Amidala. It is a luxury ship, designed for comfort rather than combat, but does have very powerful shielding in case of an attack. The vehicle is coated in royal chromium, reflecting its owner's high status.

Padmé blows up her Nubian yacht when it is captured by Separatists and taken onto their flagship, *Malevolence*.

Cockpit

Aerodynamic design for atmospheric flight

Sublight drive

SILVER MACHINE

When Padmé's yacht comes in to land, it extends three silver-colored, articulated legs. The rear of the ship then opens up to reveal a similarly shiny exit ramp.

Trip to Tatooine

Padmé's sparkling Nubian yacht makes a bold statement when it touches down on the dusty world of Tatooine. Padmé and Anakin Skywalker travel there in search of Anakin's mother.

NABOO STAR SKIFF

J-TYPE STAR SKIFF

DATA FILE

TYPE: Yacht
MANUFACTURER: Theed Palace Space Vessel Engineering Corps
SPEED: 1,050 kph (652 mph)
MODEL: J-type star skiff
HYPERDRIVE: Class 0.5
WEAPONS: 2 laser cannons

WEAPONS ON A NABOO royal ship are unheard of until this vessel is manufactured. It also has a duller, more practical, finish compared to traditional, gleaming Naboo ships. Unfortunately, the Naboo have had to adapt their ship design for the harsh realities of battle during the Clone Wars.

Senator Padmé Amidala travels in a Naboo star skiff to negotiate with crime boss Ziro the Hutt.

SHARED SHIP

The J-type star skiff is designed and built for Queen Apailana, the monarch of Naboo, in the latter days of the Clone Wars. However, the ship is also made available for Senator Padmé Amidala, the former queen.

Cockpit

Maintenance access grille

Unpolished chromium hull plating

Laser cannon

Flying into Danger

Refusing to believe that Anakin Skywalker has turned to evil, Padmé rushes to find him on the fiery world of Mustafar. She is unaware that Obi-Wan Kenobi has stowed away aboard her star skiff.

SCIMITAR

SITH INFILTRATOR

DATA FILE

TYPE: Starship
MANUFACTURER: Republic Sienar Systems
SPEED: 1,180 kph (733 mph)
MODEL: Modifed Star Courier
LENGTH: 26.5 m (86 ft 11 in)
HYPERDRIVE: Class 2
WEAPONS: 6 laser cannons, proton torpedoes

THE *SCIMITAR* IS AN experimental starcraft built—supposedly by the starship designer Raith Sienar—under orders from Darth Sidious. This sleek craft is a modified Star Courier, and it uses an experimental ion engine.

Jedi Hunting

Darth Maul uses the *Scimitar* in his mission to track down the Jedi Qui-Gon Jinn and Obi-Wan Kenobi. After Maul falls in combat with Kenobi, Darth Sidious reclaims the ship he had commissioned.

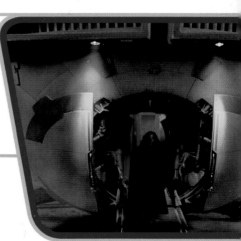

Domed cockpit

HIDDEN SHIP

The *Scimitar* can use a cloaking device to avoid detection. This ability to become invisible makes it perfect for sneaking past security and hiding from enemies.

Radiator fins release heat from experimental engines

Hidden laser cannon

The *Scimitar* carries an FC-20 speeder bike, the *Bloodfin*, in its cargo hold. This is for when Maul needs to travel quickly on land.

Heavily armored hull

SHEATHIPEDE SHUTTLE

NEIMOIDIAN ESCORT SHUTTLE

DATA FILE

TYPE: Transport
MANUFACTURER: Haor Chall Engineering
SPEED: 880 kph (546 mph)
MODEL: *Sheathipede*-class transport shuttle
LENGTH: 20 m (65 ft 7 in)
HYPERDRIVE: Equipped
WEAPONS: None

Communications antenna

Optional cockpit

Landing leg

BUILT BY INSECT-LIKE species the Charrians, the *Sheathipede*-class shuttle is used by various worlds allied to the Separatists. It is especially popular with the Neimoidians, who play a major role in the Clone Wars. These durable shuttles are used for diplomatic missions, but they can also be modified for combat.

AUTOPILOT OPTION

Some *Sheathipede*-class shuttles are flown by automatic pilots and have extra passenger or cargo space instead of a cockpit. All models have a very powerful communications array.

Time to Fly

Trade Federation leaders Nute Gunray and Rune Haako flee from the Battle of Geonosis in a *Sheathipede*-class shuttle.

Anakin Skywalker corners bio-terrorist Nuvo Vindi when he tries to escape in a Sheathipede shuttle.

SHEATHIPEDE-CLASS TYPE B

CARGO SHUTTLE

DATA FILE

TYPE: Cargo shuttle
MANUFACTURER: Haor
Chall Engineering
SPEED: 880 kph (547 mph)
MODEL: *Sheathipede*-class
Type B shuttle
HYPERDRIVE: Class 2
WEAPONS: 3 laser cannons

THE CLASS TYPE B IS A slow-moving variation of the Sheathipede shuttle, although it boasts a larger cockpit. The ship is usually reserved for transporting cargo between friendly star systems. However, during the Clone Wars, the Republic uses a shuttle to sneak into enemy territory.

Dorsal fin

Large cockpit window

ARC trooper Echo is seemingly killed when heavy fire causes his squad's stolen Class Type B shuttle to explode.

Front spotlights

Beetle-shaped chassis

Retracted landing legs

SURE-FOOTED
Designed in the shape of a soldier beetle, the shuttle uses four claw-footed legs for landing. It has three powerful lights in the front that double as a sensor array.

Frozen Solid
Anakin Skywalker, Obi-Wan Kenobi, and an elite group of clone troopers are frozen in carbonite hidden aboard a Class Type B shuttle.

SOLAR SAILER

PUNWORCCA 116-CLASS INTERSTELLAR SLOOP

THE SITH LORD COUNT DOOKU uses a solar sailer throughout the Clone Wars. The luxurious personal yacht is a rare Geonosian design with an energy-collecting sail that enables it to travel without fuel. It is fast, sleek, and surprisingly spacious, with room for Dooku's databook library inside.

DATA FILE

TYPE: Yacht
MANUFACTURER:
Huppla Pasa Tisc
Shipwrights Collective
SPEED: 1,600 kph
(994 mph)
MODEL: *Punworcca*
116-class
LENGTH: 16.7 m (54 ft 9 in)
HYPERDRIVE: Class 1.5
WEAPONS: 84 narrow
tractor/repulsor beams

Count Dooku crash-lands his solar sailer on the planet Vanqor. It falls into the hands of Weequay pirate Hondo Ohnaka, who appreciates its rarity.

Dorsal sail carapace

FA-4 pilot droid

Ventral sail carapace

Hull made from rare Geonosian metals

DEFENSE

The solar sailer's narrow-beam tractor/repulsor beams defend it from attack. When the sail is deployed, it stretches more than 100 m (328 ft) across, making a tempting and valuable target.

Sail Away

After a fierce lightsaber duel with Jedi Master Yoda, Count Dooku flees the first Battle of Geonosis. He escapes in his Punworcca 116 sloop—its solar sail fully deployed.

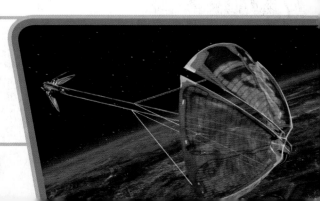

MAXILLIPEDE SHUTTLE

TRANSPORT SHUTTLE

THE MAXILLIPEDE IS ALMOST identical to the *Sheathipede*-class shuttle, but features an extra fin-like wing. This greatly increases the vessel's maneuverability in comparison to previous models, and improves long distance space travel capabilities.

DATA FILE

TYPE: Transport
MANUFACTURER: Haor Chall Engineering
SPEED: 880 kph (546 mph)
MODEL: Maxillipede shuttle
LENGTH: 14.4 m (47 ft 3 in)
HYPERDRIVE: Class 1
WEAPONS: 3 laser cannons

DROID LEADER

Colonel Meebur Gascon of the Republic, who commands a heroic group of droids known as "D-Squad," uses a captured Maxillipede shuttle.

Separatist coloring and symbol

Cockpit houses automated pilot interface

Six-passenger capacity

Clone Capture

The Separatists used a Maxillipede shuttle when attempting to capture a sick clone named Tup, who had strangely been driven to attack a Jedi Knight.

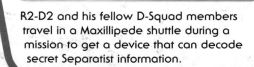

R2-D2 and his fellow D-Squad members travel in a Maxillipede shuttle during a mission to get a device that can decode secret Separatist information.

REPUBLIC ATTACK SHUTTLE

NU-CLASS TRANSPORT

WITH HEAVIER ARMOR and shielding than most atmospheric vessels, the Republic attack shuttle is a long-range alternative to the LAAT gunship. It is replaced by other shuttle designs after the Clone Wars, but one remains in the service of the rebel Cham Syndulla during the time of Empire.

DATA FILE

TYPE: Transport
MANUFACTURER: Cygnus Spaceworks
SPEED: 850 kph (528 mph)
MODEL: *Nu*-class
LENGTH: 18.9 m (62 ft)
HYPERDRIVE: Class 1
WEAPONS: 6 laser cannons

Padawan Ahsoka Tano first meets her mentor, Anakin Skywalker, after arriving on the planet Christophsis in a *Nu*-class transport.

Laser cannon

Wing hinges fold on landing

Rebel markings denote this as Cham Syndulla's ship

Cockpit

Laser cannon turret

Clone Carrier

The clone army's 212th Attack Battalion, led by Obi-Wan Kenobi, often uses *Nu*-class transports.

A TIE bomber held in the shuttle's wings

UNDER ITS WING

The Republic attack shuttle has a tractor beam, which is unusual for a transport. It also has magnetic clamps on its underside to clasp cargo and other smaller vessels. A variant *Nu*-class transport has an enclosed cargo bay built in between the wings.

T-6 SHUTTLE

JEDI AMBASSADOR SHUTTLE

DATA FILE

TYPE: Short-range shuttle fighter
MANUFACTURER: Slayn & Korpil
SPEED: 1,200 kph (745 mph)
MODEL: T-6
LENGTH: 22.8 m (74 ft 9 in)
HYPERDRIVE: Class 1
WEAPONS: None

THIS INNOVATIVE SHUTTLE DESIGN has a lasting impact on starship technology. It is built by the insectoid Verpine, and features rotating wings that allows the rest of the ship an exceptional degree of motion. Members of the Jedi Order use the shuttles frequently.

When vulture droids attack their T-6 shuttle, Ahsoka Tano and her fellow Jedi use ejector seats to launch themselves out of danger.

Three engines on main hull block

ON THE LEVEL

The shuttle's three engines and cockpit are always level with one another. When launching, the wings rotate vertically.

Ejector seats in cockpit

Wings set in landing configuration

Force Push

During a battle on the planet Toydaria, Sith apprentice Savage Opress uses the Force to shove a T-6 shuttle off a landing platform.

ETA-CLASS SHUTTLE

AMBASSADORIAL TRANSPORT

DATA FILE

TYPE: Transport
MANUFACTURER:
Cygnus Spaceworks
SPEED: 750 kph (466 mph)
MODEL: *Eta*-class shuttle
LENGTH: 14.2 m (46 ft 7 in)
HYPERDRIVE: Class 2
WEAPONS: 3 laser cannons

THESE COMFY SHUTTLES ARE first used by the Galactic Senate for diplomatic missions. Later on, they are regularly employed by the Jedi in the Clone Wars. Robust and suited to long-range travel, an *Eta*-class shuttle is chosen for a mission in Wild Space beyond the Outer Rim.

SPACIOUS SHIP

An *Eta*-class shuttle comfortably seats ten passengers and two pilots. There is also room for emergency transport, such as two *Undicar*-class jumpspeeders.

Laser cannon

Transparisteel viewport

Stability foil

Shuttle for a Sith Lord

Darth Sidious makes use of a modified *Eta*-class shuttle when he travels to the planet Mandalore to battle his former apprentice, Darth Maul.

Anakin Skywalker pilots an *Eta*-class shuttle right up to a Separatist ship to rescue the Jedi Master Eeth Koth.

H-2 EXECUTIVE SHUTTLE

LUXURY LIMOUSINE

DATA FILE

TYPE: Shuttle
MANUFACTURER: Slayn & Korpil
SPEED: 875 kph (544 mph)
MODEL: H-2 EX
LENGTH: 14.6 m (47 ft 10 in)
HYPERDRIVE: None
WEAPONS: None

THE SENATORS AND EVEN Chancellor Palpatine are among the high-profile users of this luxurious ship. Palpatine's model is docked to allow direct access from his chambers in the Senate Office Building on Coruscant. It makes for a comfy escape craft if the building is attacked.

TAKE A SEAT
The H-2 shuttle has a cockpit with a single pilot's seat and several passenger seats behind. There is plenty of room for luggage as well.

Engine air intake for atmospheric flight

Cabin door

Folding wings

Forward landing foot

Cockpit

Sliced Shuttle
When a Zillo Beast captures an H-2 shuttle with Anakin Skywalker inside, Anakin uses his lightsaber to cut the H-2 in half to escape.

Separatist senator Mina Bonteri escorts Padmé Amidala and Ahsoka Tano to her mansion aboard an H-2 shuttle.

GX1 SHORT HAULER

LANTILLIAN SHUTTLE

ORIGINALLY BUILT AS DIPLOMATIC vessels, the GX1 haulers are used as civilian transports after the Clone Wars. These vehicles are often seen traveling around the Outer Rim during the reign of the Empire.

DATA FILE

TYPE: Shuttle
MANUFACTURER: Lantillian ShipWrights
SPEED: 800 kph (497 mph)
MODEL: GX1
LENGTH: 37.2 m (122 ft)
HYPERDRIVE: Class 2
WEAPONS: Turret-mounted laser cannon

LIFE ON BOARD

Most GX1s are piloted by RX-series pilot droids. There are sleeping quarters for up to five beings, and the original GX1s even included a holo-theater for entertainment.

Long-range communications array tower

Republic colors

Secondary pod with compact hyperdrive

Need a Ride?

Young rebels Sabine Wren and Ezra Bridger are forced to flee from Imperial forces aboard a civilian GX1.

During a mission, Ahsoka Tano is knocked unconscious and wakes up on a GX1 diplomatic ship.

133

THETA-CLASS T-2C SHUTTLE

PERSONNEL TRANSPORT

DATA FILE

TYPE: Shuttlecraft
MANUFACTURER: Cygnus Spaceworks
SPEED: 2,000 kph (1,242 mph)
MODEL: Theta T-2c
LENGTH: 18.5 m (60 ft 8 in)
HYPERDRIVE: Class 1
WEAPONS: 1 laser cannon, 2 quad laser cannons

THESE SHIPS ARE BUILT by Cygnus Spaceworks, under special order by Supreme Chancellor Palpatine. They have never been available for purchase. The model is eventually incorporated into the Imperial fleet, but only for the highest-ranking officers.

Chancellor Palpatine uses this vehicle to get to the fiery planet Mustafar when he senses Anakin Skywalker is in danger there.

SHUTTLE PERKS

A center fin boosts the T-2C's ray shielding, and side wings vent heat collected by the shield. A secondary gunner station is located in the cabin.

Reinforced window to protect high-ranking passengers

Wings are raised for landing mode

Quad laser cannon

Long wings project powerful shields

Transformation

Palpatine takes a gravely injured Anakin in his T-2C shuttle to the Grand Republic Medical Facility on Coruscant. It is here that Anakin is transformed into Darth Vader.

MANDALORIAN SHUTTLE

AKA'JOR-CLASS SHUTTLE

DATA FILE

TYPE: Shuttle
MANUFACTURER:
MandalMotors
SPEED: 900 kph (559 mph)
MODEL: *Aka'jor*-class shuttle
LENGTH: 17.9 m (58 ft 8 in)
HYPERDRIVE: None
WEAPONS: None

THIS SLEEK SHIP IS BUILT by Mandalorians for Mandalorians. The *Aka'jor*-class shuttle is unarmed and intended primarily for peaceful transit between Mandalore and other planets. However, some owners have adapted their Aka'jor shuttles to carry weapons.

Rotating wing

POLICE SHIP
The Aka'jor is a highly sophisticated vehicle. The Mandalorian police force have adopted several of the ships, using them while conducting criminal investigations.

Mandalorian decoration

Cockpit window

Obi-Wan Kenobi and Duchess Satine Kryze fly in an *Aka'jor*-class shuttle when searching for signs of the Mandalorian splinter group Death Watch.

Trip to the Moon
The shuttles have rotating wings that change position during landing. They are often used to carry passengers between Mandalore and its moon, Concordia.

FLARESTAR-CLASS ATTACK SHUTTLE

WEEQUAY PIRATE SAUCER

DATA FILE

TYPE: Shuttle
MANUFACTURER: Surronian Engineering
SPEED: 1,175 kph (730 mph)
MODEL: *Flarestar*-class
LENGTH: 22.6 m (74 ft 2 in)
HYPERDRIVE: Class 2
WEAPONS: 2 laser cannons, 2 torpedo launchers

USED BY PIRATES FROM the planet Florrum, this circular ship is launched out of a much larger saucer, acting as a landing craft. The shuttles can also function on their own, repurposed into fast and powerful fighters.

The pirate Barb Mentir uses a *Flarestar*-class attack shuttle to attack a Republic vessel carrying Jar Jar Binks.

One of two cockpits

Hondo Ohnaka's pirate symbol

Maul Aboard

When Darth Maul and Savage Opress board a *Flarestar*-class attack shuttle, they force its pirate crew to join Maul's new criminal enterprise.

SAUCERFUL OF PIRATES

Despite its dual cockpits, the shuttle can be operated by a single pilot. It has room for three crew and ten passengers.

TAYLANDER SHUTTLE

CIVILIAN TRANSPORT SHUTTLE

DATA FILE

TYPE: Shuttle
MANUFACTURER: Gallofree Yards, Inc.
SPEED: 950 kph (590 mph)
MODEL: Taylander
LENGTH: 43.5 m (142 ft 8 in)
HYPERDRIVE: Class 2
WEAPONS: None

THE TAYLANDER SHUTTLES ARE civilian transport vehicles prevalent during the final years of the Republic. They are a common sight amongst the peaceful Core Worlds, but are even found in the far reaches of the Outer Rim.

After the Empire rises to power, rebel forces begin acquiring Taylander shuttles to use for transport on populated worlds.

Aerodynamic fins

Heavily armored hull

Rounded bow

Docking bay

ARMORED VEHICLE

Each Taylander shuttle has heavy armor to make up for its lack of weaponry. It also has three landing struts that deploy as needed.

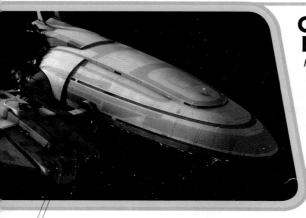

Close Escape

Mon Mothma's Taylander shuttle, the *Chandrila Mistress*, is attacked by Imperial forces. Luckily, the rebel leader is able to escape on Hera Syndulla's ship, the *Ghost*.

PHANTOM

MODIFIED VCX-SERIES AUXILIARY STARFIGHTER

DATA FILE

TYPE: Short-range Corellian shuttle fighter
MANUFACTURER: Corellian Engineering Corporation
SPEED: 1,200 kph (746 mph)
MODEL: Modified VCX-series auxiliary starfighter
LENGTH: 11.6 m (38 ft)
HYPERDRIVE: Class 1
WEAPONS: 1 twin laser cannon, 1 laser turret

DESIGNED TO DOCK WITH the Corellian VCX light freighter, the VCX-series auxiliary starfighter is an effective shuttle and a versatile combat ship. The *Phantom* is a modified version used by the rebel crew of the VCX freighter known as the *Ghost*.

Laser turret

Cockpit

Twin laser cannon

Design by Sabine Wren

PHANTOM MENACE

The *Phantom* has been upgraded with salvaged parts to make it more of a threat in battle. Its cockpit comes from another kind of starfighter, and it has been equipped with a hyperdrive.

Calling all Creatures

Hera Syndulla realizes that the *Phantom*'s jamming signal attracts the tibidees' attention. When Hera picks up her rebel team from an Imperial prison, she uses the creatures as cover.

The *Phantom* is attacked by a dismantler droid, then destroyed, during a raid to steal Y-wings from an Imperial scrapyard.

PHANTOM II

MODIFIED *SHEATHIPEDE*-CLASS SHUTTLE

DATA FILE

TYPE: Transport
MANUFACTURER: Haor Chall Engineering
SPEED: 1,250 kph (777 mph)
MODEL: Modified *Sheathipede*-class shuttle
LENGTH: 14.4 m (47 ft 3 in)
HYPERDRIVE: Equipped
WEAPONS: 2 forward-mounted cannons, 2 rear ventral turrets

FOLLOWING THE DESTRUCTION of their original short-range shuttle, the rebel crew of the *Ghost* adapt an old Clone Wars-era vessel to become the *Phantom II*. The *Sheathipede*-class shuttle is also given a new color scheme by Sabine Wren.

Design by rebel Sabine Wren

MOD POD

The modified *Phantom II* is much faster and far more durable than a traditional *Sheathipede*-class shuttle. It is also equipped with heavy weapons and an astromech port.

Forward cannon

Chopper in astromech port

Retracted landing leg

Doctored Dock

When the rebels upgrade the shuttle to become the *Phantom II*, they modify it to fit into the same docking port as the original *Phantom* at the rear of their VCX-100 light freighter, the *Ghost*.

When the rebels seek an alliance with the Mandalorian Clan Wren, the clan shoots the *Phantom II* down.

STAR COMMUTER 2000

SHORT-RANGE SHUTTLE

RX-SERIES DROIDS pilot these civilian shuttles, which are designed to provide quick, comfy travel between neighboring worlds. They are also used to ferry visitors to and from larger ships in orbit of planets and space stations.

Stolen Shuttle

Stormtroopers fire on a Star Commuter 2000 when it is stolen by rebels trying to save a rebel sympathizer from being imprisoned.

Corporate color scheme varies between routes

Forward viewports

Passenger viewport

The crew of the *Ghost* book passage on a Star Commuter to get close to a high-ranking Imperial official aboard.

Boarding hatch

BOARDING PROCEDURE

Passengers can board the Star Commuter 2000 on either side, and sit in two rows of double seats with safety belts. Droids are required to stand at the back of the ship.

DELTA-CLASS T-3C SHUTTLE

DIRECTOR KRENNIC'S PERSONAL SHUTTLE

DATA FILE

TYPE: Shuttle
MANUFACTURER: Sienar Fleet Systems
SPEED: 1,000 kph (621 mph)
MODEL: *Delta*-class T-3c
LENGTH: 14.4 m (47 ft 2 in)
HYPERDRIVE: Class 1
WEAPONS: 2 twin laser cannons, 3 wing laser cannons

Cockpit window

THE SLEEK AND STEALTHY

Delta-class T-3c is never put into full production. However, one prototype of the unique shuttle is built specifically for Orson Callan Krennic, Director of the construction of the first Death Star. The shuttle is enhanced for stealth and features a sloped hull with folding lateral wings that minimize its footprint on the ground.

Twin laser cannons

BASIC NEEDS

The shuttle's interior is sparse and functional, with basic crash seats and storage straps. The ship's communications equipment is built into the wings.

Krennic's shuttle lands on the planet Lah'mu, outside the homestead of former Imperial scientist Galen Erso.

Sleek, folding wings

Visiting a Sith

The *Delta*-class T-3c carries Director Krennic to Darth Vader's stronghold on the burning world of Mustafar. It is a meeting that the Director is lucky to survive!

LAMBDA-CLASS SHUTTLE

IMPERIAL SHUTTLE

DATA FILE

TYPE: Shuttle
MANUFACTURER: Sienar Fleet Systems
SPEED: 850 kph (528 mph)
MODEL: *Lambda*-class T-4a
LENGTH: 20 m (65 ft 7 in)
HYPERDRIVE: Class 1
WEAPONS: 2 forward-facing laser cannons, 2 twin wing-mounted laser cannons, 1 retractable rear-mounted double laser cannon

Dorsal stabilizer wing

THE T-4A SHUTTLE IS an unusually sleek craft compared to the typically plain and practical designs preferred by the Empire. The ship transports troops in non-combat situations, and is available for private use by high-ranking Imperial officials and dignitaries.

Luke Skywalker, Han Solo, Leia Organa, and Chewbacca use a stolen shuttle to sneak onto Endor's moon. Darth Vader senses Luke's presence aboard.

Twin wing-mounted laser cannon

SAFE SHUTTLE

A single pilot can control the T-4a, but a co-pilot is usually assigned. The lower wings fold upward upon landing. The cockpit also becomes a lifeboat in emergencies.

Wide cockpit window

Emperor's Ship

When the Emperor arrives on the second Death Star, he is brought aboard by his personal *Lambda*-class T-4a shuttle. It is easily identified by a gray stripe that runs down the front of the ship.

SENTINEL-CLASS SHUTTLE

IMPERIAL LANDING CRAFT

DATA FILE

TYPE: Shuttle
MANUFACTURER: Sienar Fleet Systems
SPEED: 1,000 kph (621 mph)
MODEL: *Sentinel*-class
LENGTH: 38 m (124 ft 8 in)
HYPERDRIVE: Class 1
WEAPONS: 8 laser cannons, 2 concussion missile launchers, 2 blaster cannon turrets, ion cannon turret

MUCH LARGER THAN THE similar-looking *Lambda*-class T-4A shuttle, this Imperial lander is a troop transporter. It is equipped with heavy weapons and has space aboard for 54 stormtroopers. A cargo pod can be installed on the shuttle's underside to house attack vehicles.

INTO BATTLE

The *Sentinel*-class shuttle is equipped with powerful shields for delivering stormtroopers into the thick of battle. Troops can deploy from all four sides of the vessel for maximum flexibility.

Cockpit viewport

Hinges for folding wings

Retractable laser cannon hatch

Forward ramp

Tarkin is in

Grand Moff Tarkin's *Sentinel*-class shuttle arrives at the Imperial Complex docking bay on Lothal, its wings folding as it lands.

Jedi Kanan Jarrus and clone captain Rex use a *Sentinel*-class shuttle to sneak onto another Imperial ship.

ZETA-CLASS CARGO SHUTTLE

IMPERIAL COURIER CRAFT

DATA FILE

TYPE: Shuttle
MANUFACTURER: Sienar
Fleet Systems/Telgorn
Corporation
SPEED: 1,000 kph
(621 mph)
MODEL: *Zeta*-class
LENGTH: 35.5 m (116 ft 6 in)
HYPERDRIVE: Class 1
WEAPONS: 3 twin laser
cannons, 2 twin heavy
laser cannons

THE *ZETA*-CLASS CARGO shuttle is not designed for combat, but it has to be well armed to protect the precious shipments it often carries. Its pilots rarely see battle however, and spend most of their days chasing security clearance.

Wings fold
down during flight

Heavy laser
cannon

Primary
sensor bay

Hydraulic ramp

Cargo deck

HEAVY DUTY

A *Zeta*-class cargo shuttle can carry up to 25 metric tons (55,116 lbs) of freight in a detachable cargo deck. It can be adapted for use as a passenger transport.

Crystal Carrier

The Imperial occupation of the planet Jedha sees *Zeta*-class shuttles used to transport kyber crystals from Jedha City to a refinery on the world of Eadu.

A band of rebels led by Jyn Erso uses *Zeta*-class shuttle SW-0608 to infiltrate the base where the Death Star plans are stored.

UPSILON-CLASS SHUTTLE

FIRST ORDER TRANSPORT

DATA FILE

TYPE: Shuttle
MANUFACTURER: Sienar-Jaemus Fleet Systems
SPEED: 950 kph (590 mph)
MODEL: *Upsilon*-class
LENGTH: 19.1 m (62 ft 7 in)
HYPERDRIVE: Class 1
WEAPONS: 2 twin heavy laser cannons

THIS SHUTTLE IS RESERVED for Kylo Ren and other high-ranking members of the First Order. Inspired by Imperial era shuttles, its large, folding wings provide cover from enemy fire during takeoff and landing. Advanced sensor-jamming technology makes the ship hard to detect in flight.

Stepping Out

Kylo Ren arrives on the planet Jakku in his personal *Upsilon*-class shuttle, flanked by a pair of First Order stormtroopers.

Finn has a bad feeling when he sees an *Upsilon*-class shuttle landing on the planet Takodana.

STEALTH SHUTTLE

Designed for stealth rather than strength, the *Upsilon*-class shuttle has few weapons. Instead, it excels in collecting detailed sensor data. This allows it to stay two steps ahead of its New Republic and Resistance enemies at all times.

Passenger compartment

Durasteel armor

Cockpit

Twin heavy laser cannon

SLAVE I

BOUNTY HUNTER'S VESSEL

DATA FILE

TYPE: Pursuit vessel
MANUFACTURER: Kuat Systems Engineering
SPEED: 1,000 kph (621 mph)
MODEL: *Firespray*-class patrol and attack craft
LENGTH: 21.5 m (70 ft 6 in)
HYPERDRIVE: Class 2
WEAPONS: Twin rotating blaster cannons, laser cannons, ion cannon, seismic charges, concussion missiles

ONE OF THE MOST dangerous ships in the galaxy, *Slave I* is the private vessel of the much-feared bounty hunter Jango Fett. *Slave I*'s controls are heavily modified to make it responsive enough to match the flying pattern of any other ship.

COMPLEX CRAFT

Slave I is a sophisticated ship that requires a highly experienced pilot. It is equipped with experimental sensor disruptors and its wings work as repulsorlifts.

Stabilizer fin

Cockpit energy shield

Oval hull

Hondo Ohnaka uses *Slave I* to escape General Grievous's forces.

Rotating blaster cannon

Family Business

Jango Fett's son, Boba, continues his father's work. During the Galactic Civil War, he uses *Slave I* to hunt down the *Millennium Falcon* for Darth Vader.

TWILIGHT

CORELLIAN G9 RIGGER FREIGHTER

DATA FILE

TYPE: Freighter
MANUFACTURER: Corellian Engineering Corporation
SPEED: 700 kph (435 mph)
MODEL: G9 *Rigger*-class light freighter
LENGTH: 34 m (111 ft 1 in)
HYPERDRIVE: Class 3
WEAPONS: 3 heavy blasters, rotating laser cannon

THE *TWILIGHT* IS originally the property of crime lord Ziro Desilijic Tiure. It is later claimed by Anakin Skywalker, who puts it to use during the Clone Wars. This old ship is considered massively out of date, so Anakin spends a large amount of his free time upgrading the vehicle.

Anakin and Ahsoka Tano fly the *Twilight* in pursuit of Cad Bane after he kidnaps several Force-sensitive children.

Cockpit between engine and main wing

Double heavy blaster cannon

Single, fixed main wing

Rotating laser cannon

Folding swing-wing with blaster cannon

To the Rescue

Master Plo Koon's ship is destroyed by the *Malevolence*. Anakin and Ahsoka use the *Twilight* to rescue him and several clone troopers from an escape pod.

UNIQUE SHIP

The side of the *Twilight* is decorated with a cartoonish painting of young Anakin podracing. The ship's upgraded weapons system causes random color shifts in the lasers.

HALO

SS-54 ASSAULT SHIP

THE FEARSOME bounty hunter Sugi commands this well-armed vessel during the Clone Wars. She uses it to carry out mercenary missions on behalf of anyone willing to pay her danger money.

The *Halo*'s scary tooka-doll mascot doesn't faze the Wookiee soldiers who team up with Sugi.

DATA FILE

TYPE: Gunship
MANUFACTURER: Botajef Shipyards
SPEED: 800 kph (497 mph)
MODEL: SS-54
LENGTH: 24.2 m (79 ft 5 in)
HYPERDRIVE: Class 1
WEAPONS: 2 twin laser cannons, 1 dual laser cannon

PARTING SHOTS

The *Halo* has a powerful aft-facing dual laser cannon at the rear for fending off pursuers. It is larger than the forward-mounted cannons.

Cockpit viewport

Engines rotate 90 degrees for take off and landing

Deployment hatch

Twin laser cannon

Home by *Halo*

Sugi works with Obi-Wan Kenobi, Anakin Skywalker, and Ahsoka Tano to protect a village from Hondo Ohnaka's pirate gang. She then offers the Jedi passage home aboard the *Halo*.

HOUND'S TOOTH

YV-666 LIGHT FREIGHTER

DATA FILE

TYPE: Light freighter
MANUFACTURER: Corellian Engineering Corporation
SPEED: 1,190 kph (739 mph)
MODEL: Modified YV-666
LENGTH: 47.4 m (155 ft 6 in)
HYPERDRIVE: Class 1.5
WEAPONS: 1 quad laser cannon turret, 1 ion cannon, 1 concussion missile launcher

BOUNTY HUNTER BOSSK uses this ordinary-looking freighter for his far-from-ordinary work. It is home to the Trandoshan's huge collection of weapons and interrogation tools, plus a gruesome array of trophies from his many years as a hunter for hire.

NO WAY OUT
Bossk has turned the cargo bays of the *Hound's Tooth* into high-security cells for his prisoners. The ship also has an advanced security system, so even if anyone does succeed in breaking out—or in—they won't get far without being blasted!

Command bridge viewport

Maneuvering fin

Side ramp

Deflector shield generator

Cruel Cargo
The *Hound's Tooth* docks at an orbital elevator station, where Bossk and his fellow bounty hunters will pick up a valuable cargo. This cargo turns out to be a young woman named Pluma Sodi!

Painted mascot

Forward ramp

Bossk pilots the *Hound's Tooth* with a band of bounty hunters, including a young Boba Fett.

TURTLE TANKER

TRANSPORT/WALKER HYBRID

DATA FILE

TYPE: Transport/walker
MANUFACTURER: Corellia Mining Corporation
SPEED: 750 kph (466 mph)
MODEL: Goji-DF
LENGTH: 38 m (124 ft 8 in)
WEAPONS: None

ORIGINALLY DESIGNED TO HAUL minerals from asteroid mines, the bulk tankers (commonly known as "Turtle Tankers") are cheap and easy to build. This makes them a familiar sight in established space lanes. However, their lack of weaponry makes them a rare choice outside of heavily trafficked areas.

Blue running lights

MULTI-PURPOSE
A Turtle Tanker's hold is divided to accommodate different types of cargo. The cockpit doubles as an escape pod and the landing gear doubles as its legs.

Entrance to tanker's hold

Cockpit also functions as escape pod

All-terrain walker legs

Loading ramp

Evil Intentions
Brothers Darth Maul and Savage Opress hijack a Turtle Tanker. After piloting it to the planet Raydonia, they destroy the peaceful inhabitants of a settlement.

Opress and Maul's Turtle Tanker becomes a battleground when they face Obi-Wan Kenobi and Asajj Ventress in the cargo hold.

MOOGAN GUNSHIP

SHEKELESH-CLASS FREIGHT GUNSHIP

DATA FILE

TYPE: Freight gunship
MANUFACTURER:
Techno Union
SPEED: 300 kph (186 mph)
MODEL: *Shekelesh*-class
HEIGHT: 21.1 m (69 ft 2 in)
HYPERDRIVE: Class 1
WEAPONS: 2 twin laser cannons

THESE ODD-LOOKING CRAFT are built by the Separatist-supporting Techo Union, but they are best known as Moogan smugglers' ships. With a narrow cargo hold and small, awkward legs, it is unsurprising they are not very popular.

Sensor antenna

Viewport

LEG IT!

The landing legs of the *Shekelesh*-class freight gunship allow the vessel to act as a rudimentary walker. It scuttles its way around freight yards, avoiding any customs officials!

Duchess Satine Kryze spies on a ring of smugglers as they unload their Moogan gunship by night.

Laser cannons

Trouble Brewing

During the Clone Wars, Moogan smugglers on the planet Mandalore distribute poisonous tea from a *Shekelesh*-class freight gunship.

Moogan smuggler

Loading ramp

One of six legs

Gotal smuggler

PANTORAN CRUISER

RAINHAWK-CLASS TRANSPORT

THE PANTORAN CRUISER IS a sturdy ship that favors defense over offense. Powerful engines and repulsor technology enable it to outmaneuver most standard fighters—but not to outrun them. It is largely discontinued by the time of the Clone Wars.

Transparisteel cockpit window

Tail fin adds stability during atmospheric flight

Laser cannon

FOR TWO

The cockpit of the Pantoran cruiser seats two, and there are two small bunks inside the ship for long journeys. A ladder leads down from the cockpit to the ship's hatch.

Ion engine

Familiar Sight

Chairman Papanoida's Pantoran cruiser is regularly seen outside the Senate building on Coruscant. It is stationed directly next to the landing platform reserved for the Naboo.

Papanoida and his son, Ion, travel on a Pantoran cruiser named the *Falfa*. They fly it to Tatooine to find the bounty hunter who attacked their family.

GHOST

REBEL FREIGHTER

DATA FILE

TYPE: Light freighter
MANUFACTURER: Corellian
Engineering Corporation
SPEED: 1,025 kph (637 mph)
MODEL: VCX-100 (modified)
LENGTH: 43.9 m (144 ft)
HYPERDRIVE: Class 2
WEAPONS: 1 twin laser
cannon, 2 laser
cannon turrets,
2 proton torpedo
launchers

THE *GHOST* IS FAST
and light, and has seen
more than its fair share
of battle. Owned by Hera
Syndulla and serving as
a mobile home for a
small band of rebels, this
modified freighter is high
on the Empire's wanted list.

Commander Jun Sato's ship is
caught in an Imperial tractor
beam. Hera pilots the *Ghost*
directly into the path of the
beam and disables it.

Laser cannon
turret

Docking ring

Old scuff marks
from battle

Cockpit

Perfect Pilot

No one could fly the *Ghost* better
than its owner, Hera Sydulla. She is
one of the best pilots in the Rebel
Alliance! Her incredible flying skills
have led to victories on many rebel
missions and in numerous battles.

THE ARTIST

Rebel Sabine Wren
decorates the interior
of the *Ghost* with her
colorful artwork. This
makes the ship feel
more like home.

LANCER-CLASS PURSUIT CRAFT

UNDERGROUND TRANSPORT CRAFT

DATA FILE

TYPE: Transport/pursuit craft
MANUFACTURER:
MandalMotors
SPEED: 1,050 kph (652 mph)
MODEL: *Lancer*-class
LENGTH: 18 m (59 ft)
HYPERDRIVE: Class 1
WEAPONS: 1 triple laser turret,
4 laser cannons

CREATED BY MANDALMOTORS,
the *Lancer*-class pursuit craft is a
versatile and well-armed ship.
It boasts a powerful twin-engine
system and a tractor beam
projector. Unsurprisingly,
it becomes a popular vessel
with bounty hunters, including
Asajj Ventress and Ketsu Onyo.

LIVE-IN SHIP

While it may not be the
most attractive ship,
the *Lancer*-class pursuit
craft has basic living
quarters. It contains two
cosy cabins, a compact
kitchen, one bathroom,
and a cargo hold.

Triple laser
turret

Disk-like
shape

Powerful twin
engines

Forward laser
cannons

Long, narrow
cockpit

Special Delivery
Ketsu and Sabine use the *Shadow Caster* to
transport a droid (that holds secret information)
to a rebel leader named Bail Organa.

Sabine Wren's former friend, Ketsu
Onyo, flies a *Lancer*-class ship
named the *Shadow Caster*
while working for the Black Sun.

YT-2400 LIGHT FREIGHTER

DATA FILE

TYPE: Light freighter
MANUFACTURER: Corellian Engineering Corporation
SPEED: 800 kph (497 mph)
MODEL: YT-2400
LENGTH: 21 m (68 ft 10 in)
HYPERDRIVE: Class 2
WEAPONS: 2 double laser turrets, concussion missile launchers

THE YT-2400 IS A popular choice for cargo haulers and pirates alike, due to its high speed and maneuverability. The ship is also used by members of a rebel cell named Iron Squadron.

Double laser turret

Two layers of armor plate

Primary cargo hold

Cylindrical cockpit

Six-seater escape pod

LAYOUT
The YT-2400 has quarters for five crew, but only one pilot is required to fly the ship. An escape pod is located just behind the cockpit.

Young Rebels
A rebel cell known as Iron Squadron flies a YT-2400 named *Sato's Hammer* on raids against the Empire in the Mykapo system. Its young members include Mart Mattin, Jonner Jin, Gooti Terez, and a droid named R3-A3.

During a space battle, Iron Squadron drops some cargo on an Imperial cruiser, causing it to explode!

MILLENNIUM FALCON

SMUGGLER FREIGHTER

THE *MILLENNIUM FALCON* LIVES up to its reputation as "the fastest ship in the galaxy," despite its numerous modifications and repairs over the years. Its rough and ready appearance lead many people to underestimate its formidable capabilities.

DATA FILE

TYPE: Light freighter
MANUFACTURER: Corellian Engineering Corporation
SPEED: 1,050 kph (652 mph)
MODEL: YT-1300f light freighter
LENGTH: 34.5 m (113 ft 2 in)
HYPERDRIVE: Class 0.5
WEAPONS: 2 quad laser cannons, concussion missiles, undercarriage blaster cannon, tractor beam projectors

Cockpit seats four

Power core

Sensor dish

Front-facing twin mandibles

Tractor beam projector

SHIP OF SECRETS
Han Solo wins the *Falcon* from his old friend Lando Calrissian in a game of Sabacc. He soon modifies the ship to suit his smuggling needs. There are now multiple hidden compartments within the hull.

Flyboy
Han Solo and his friend Chewbacca use the freighter as a smuggling ship. Han becomes infamous for his reckless flying.

The *Falcon* is eventually stolen from Han. It has many owners before ending up on Jakku, where it is stolen by a young scavenger named Rey.

DORNEAN GUNSHIP

BRAHA'TOK-CLASS GUNSHIP

DATA FILE

TYPE: Gunship
MANUFACTURER: Dornean
Braha'ket Fleetworks
Conglomorate
SPEED: 800 kph (497 mph)
MODEL: *Braha'tok*-class
LENGTH: 90 m (295 ft 3 in)
HYPERDRIVE: Class 1
WEAPONS: 8 turbolasers,
8 concussion missiles

THESE GUNSHIPS ARE CREATED to protect the Dornean homeworld from the Empire. They may be small, but they are designed specifically to counter large groups of enemy fighters. These gunships are a valuable addition to any battle!

A Dornean gunship serves in the rebel fleet during the Battle of Scarif. When an Imperial Star Destroyer exits hyperspace, the gunship narrowly avoids a collision and escapes.

Command bridge located in ship's bow

Hyperdrive

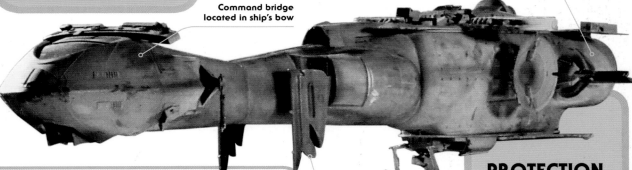

PROTECTION

The Dornean gunship uses silver plating to deflect solar radiation. It can carry a crew of 75, and two X-wings can be mounted on its undercarriage.

Joining the Fleet

When Grand Admiral Thrawn launches his first major attack against the rebel forces, three Dornean gunships serve as part of the defense of Attolon.

X-wing attachment clip

REPUBLIC TUGBOAT

INTERSTELLAR TUG

REPUBLIC TUGBOATS ARE USED during the Clone Wars to maneuver massive warships into docking ports at space stations. These tugboats are low on shields and have no weapons, but are equipped with powerful engines and tractor beams.

Short-range communications tower

After the Kaliida Shoals Medical Center is refurbished by the Republic, tugboats transport it to its new home.

Wide-angle view limits blindspots

Oversized engines in proportion to ship

Hard Stop

When the crew of a Republic frigate is compromised with mind-controlling brain worms, two tugboats are needed to stop the runaway vehicle.

Tractor beams guide larger craft

MULTI-FUNCTIONAL

Each tugboat also serves as an emergency vehicle, with fire-fighting equipment and salvage scanners.

QUADJUMPER

QUADRIJET TRANSFER SPACETUG

DATA FILE

TYPE: Spacetug
MANUFACTURER: Subpro
SPEED: 1,150 kph
(714 mph)
MODEL: TUG-b13
LENGTH: 7.9 m (25 ft 11 in)
HYPERDRIVE: None
WEAPONS: None

THIS CARGO TUG consists of a small cabin surrounded by large thrusters. Designed to shunt freight containers in orbital transfer yards, the quadjumper uses a magnetic clamp to haul loads far larger than the ship itself.

Second Time Lucky

As the First Order attacks Niima Outpost on the planet Jakku, Rey and Finn try to escape in a quadjumper. When the ship is blown up by a TIE fighter, they opt for the *Millennium Falcon* instead.

Heat exchanger plate

Thruster casing

Stabilizer vane

Cockpit

Hydraulic landing gear

Jakku trader Unkar Plutt acquires an unmodifed quadjumper from arms dealers he has yet to pay.

THE MOD QUAD

Quadjumpers are easily modified with weapons and extra fuel tanks. They can also be configured to have a hyperdrive. This makes them a popular choice for mineral prospectors and smugglers.

AA-9 CORUSCANT FREIGHTER

BOTAJEF FREIGHTER-LINER

DATA FILE

TYPE: Freighter
MANUFACTURER: Botajef
Shipyards
SPEED: 420 kph (261 mph)
MODEL: Botajef AA-9
Freighter-Liner
LENGTH: 390 m
(1,279 ft 6 in)
HYPERDRIVE: Class 4
WEAPONS: None

THE AA-9 CORUSCANT FREIGHTERS are originally built to haul cargo. During the war with the Separatists, the Refugee Relief Movement has them transformed into vessels that can help people in need. The freighters transport refugees from planets that have fallen under enemy control.

Powerful engines

Boarding area

Multi-deck accommodation

After an attack on her life, Padmé Amidala secretly travels to Naboo in an AA-9 called the *Jendirian Valley*.

Prime Location

Many AA-9s are used by the Grand Army of the Republic during the Clone Wars. Their location on Coruscant makes them ideal for transporting cargo and clone troopers.

PEOPLE CARRIER

In an emergency, the AA-9 can hold up to 30,000 life forms. There are over three months worth of emergency supplies aboard.

ZYGERRIAN SLAVE SHIP

AURORE-CLASS FREIGHTER

DATA FILE

TYPE: Freighter
MANUFACTURER: Corellian Engineering Corporation
SPEED: 900 kph (559 mph)
MODEL: YV-865
LENGTH: 52.3 m (171 ft 7 in)
HYPERDRIVE: Class 1
WEAPONS: Twin forward-mounted medium laser cannons

THE AURORE-CLASS FREIGHTERS are spacious cargo ships. They are a favorite amongst the Zygerrian slavers because they can hold a large number of prisoners while only requiring one pilot. This soon makes them unpopular with other cultures.

NO ESCAPE
The Aurore-class freighter cargo hold can be packed with up to 100 slaves. However, there is only one escape pod aboard.

Cockpit with geometric windows

Huge hold for large amounts of live cargo

Thruster engine on boom arm

Inter-Galactic Circus

An Aurore-class freighter becomes the home of Preigo's Traveling World of Wonder. This circus performs entertaining shows on many worlds across the galaxy.

When Anakin Skywalker and Ahsoka Tano land an Aurore-class freighter at the Kadavo prison, the security system blows it up!

VULTURE'S CLAW

GS-100 SALVAGE SHIP

DATA FILE

TYPE: Salvage Ship
MANUFACTURER: Gallofree Yards, Inc.
SPEED: 400 kph (248 mph)
MODEL: GS-100
LENGTH: 174.8 m (573 ft 5 in)
HYPERDRIVE: Class 3
WEAPONS: Torpedoes, dual laser cannon

THE *VULTURE'S CLAW* IS a common sight in the Mid Rim for many years. It is often seen after a battle, sifting through debris in search of valuable items to resell. Finds are taken into the ship's interior, which serves as one-half junk yard and one-half shop.

While aboard the *Vulture's Claw*, Anakin Skywalker and Ahsoka Tano are ambushed by IG-86 assassin droids.

Dual laser cannon turret

Pincers for picking up wreckage

Multi-spectrum spotlight

Holds for storing and processing debris

Lost and Found

After R2-D2 is seemingly lost in the Battle of Bothawui, the Trandoshan junk dealer known as Gha Nachkt finds the droid among the ruins.

HEAVY LIFTING

This ship can carry up to 140 metric tons of debris. It has many retractable arms for sifting space debris. Four engines power the ship, though it can run on just one.

IMPERIAL FREIGHTER

GOZANTI-CLASS CRUISER

DATA FILE

TYPE: Cruiser
MANUFACTURER: Corellian Engineering Corporation
SPEED: 1,025 kph (636 mph)
MODEL: *Gozanti*-class
LENGTH: 63.8 m (209 ft 4 in)
HYPERDRIVE: Class 3
WEAPONS: Twin laser cannon turret, heavy laser cannon turret

HEAVILY SHIELDED AND WELL armed, this cruiser is used by the Separatists and the Black Sun crime syndicate during the Clone Wars. Later, it becomes known as an Imperial freighter, deploying TIE fighters, AT-DPs, and even AT-AT walkers into battle. The vessels also serve as standard supply ships and prisoner transports.

UNDER STUDY

The Empire's *Gozanti*-class cruisers have been converted for military use. They possess stronger shields, quicker engines, and better weapons than other types of Gozanti cruisers. They can also mount other ships on their underside.

Shield projector

Twin laser cannon turret

Command bridge viewport

TIE fighters on docking struts

Back in the Day

A *Gozanti*-class cruiser flies over the Mos Espa spaceport on Tatooine in the latter years of the Galactic Republic.

Imperial forces disembark from a *Gozanti*-class cruiser (using the cargo loading elevator) on the planet Lothal.

IGV-55 SURVEILLANCE VESSEL

IMPERIAL LISTENER SHIP

DATA FILE

TYPE: Espionage ship
MANUFACTURER: Corellian Engineering Corporation
SPEED: 900 kph (559 mph)
MODEL: Modified *Gozanti*-class espionage ship
LENGTH: 64 m (209 ft 11 in)
HYPERDRIVE: Class 1
WEAPONS: 2 heavy laser cannons

THE IGV-55 MODEL OF ship is never seen as part of an Imperial fleet. Instead, these espionage ships are typically positioned in deep space, far from traditional traffic lanes. There, they use their powerful receivers to scan for information helpful to the Imperial cause.

The IGV-55 is run by a cybernetic controller, and is staffed with the best Imperial intelligence officers.

INTELLIGENCE VESSEL

Multiple sensor dishes allow the ships to listen for light years in any direction, and all four engines are outfitted with sensor-dampening encasements. A massive database is built into the core of the ship, to store billions of yottabytes of data.

Long-range transmitter dish

Viewing and command deck

Sensory array

Heavy laser cannon

Modified, rear-mounted quad engines

Ready to Serve

Hera Syndulla discovers that the crew of an IGV-55 is trying to take control of her astromech droid, Chopper. She sends a powerful signal back to the IGV-55, which causes its systems to overload.

IMPERIAL CARGO SHIP

CLASS FOUR CONTAINER TRANSPORT

DATA FILE

TYPE: Freighter
MANUFACTURER: Kuat Drive Yards
SPEED: 700 kph (435 mph)
MODEL: Class 4 CT
LENGTH: 233 m (764 ft 5 in)
HYPERDRIVE: Class 1
WEAPONS: 2 laser turrets, turbolaser battery

PULLING MORE THAN 200 cargo containers at any one time, these large, pyramid-shaped ships transport vital supplies around the Empire. This makes them tempting targets for smugglers and rebels, but their distinctive shape makes it impossible to pass stolen cargo ships off as private vessels.

AT THE BACK

The class four container transport has three sublight engines, one located in each corner of the back surface. Its cargo containers attach between these engines, where a hatch allows easy crew access to the train of cargo.

Turbolaser battery

Laser turret

Command bridge

Armored hull

Bay Watch

Some class four container transports have a docking bay built into the cargo train. The *Ghost* crew use this to its advantage when they set out to hijack a fully loaded Imperial cargo ship.

Every Imperial cargo ship has its own inventory droid. The rebel droid Chopper convinces one such droid, AP-5, to swap sides!

BROKEN HORN

C-ROC *GOZANTI*-CLASS CRUISER

DATA FILE

TYPE: Cruiser
MANUFACTURER: Corellian Engineering Corporation
MODEL: Modified C-ROC *Gozanti*-class
LENGTH: 73.9 m (242 ft 5 in)
HYPERDRIVE: Class 3
WEAPONS: 1 dorsal laser turret, 2 forward laser cannons, 2 rear laser cannons

CRIME KINGPIN Cikatro Vizago runs the shady Broken Horn Syndicate from this ship—a C-ROC *Gozanti*-class cruiser that has been transformed into a smuggler's stronghold. What it lacks in weapons it makes up for with shields and speed. The *Broken Horn* can get out of almost any unwanted encounter.

Hondo's *Horn*

When Ezra Bridger and Chopper respond to a distress call, they find the *Broken Horn* adrift in space and seemingly abandoned. In fact, the pirate Hondo Ohnaka is aboard, and claiming the ship as his own!

Sensor dish

Cargo containers

Command bridge

Twin engine turbines

Broken Horn Syndicate symbol

As part of a mission to save Kanan Jarrus, Ezra Bridger meets with Vizago aboard the *Broken Horn*.

HORN OF PLENTY

The *Broken Horn* has plenty of interior cargo space, but adds to its capacity with a large freight platform on either side.

ERAVANA

BALEEN-CLASS HEAVY FREIGHTER

DATA FILE

TYPE: Bulk freighter
MANUFACTURER: Corellian Engineering Corporation
SPEED: 750 kph (466 mph)
MODEL: *Baleen*-class
LENGTH: 426 m (1,397 ft 7 in)
HYPERDRIVE: Class 2
WEAPONS: None

AFTER HAN SOLO LOSES the *Millennium Falcon*, the *Eravana* becomes his new ship. A heavy freighter for hauling cargo, its front section opens like a mouth to salvage space debris, while its rear is a grid of cargo pods. It is unsophisticated, but suitable for smuggling.

Rey and Finn meet Han and Chewbacca when Han detects his lost ship, the *Millennium Falcon,* and brings it aboard the *Eravana.*

Cargo pods

Docking bay repressurization system

Container transport grid

Observation deck

Docking bay

Later, Freighter

Han, Chewbacca, Rey, Finn, and BB-8 are forced to flee the *Eravana* on the *Falcon*. They leave behind two rival gangs and three wild rathtars fighting in the freighter!

HEAVY HAULAGE

Baleen-class heavy freighters are not designed to land on planets. They are built in orbit and spend their days hauling cargo pods to and from space stations where their cargo can be redistributed.

NABOO ROYAL STARSHIP

MODIFIED J-TYPE 327 NUBIAN STARSHIP

THIS SLEEK SHIP IS CRAFTED to be a visual representation of the glory of Naboo. It has no weapons, but it is equipped with state-of-the-art deflector shields in case of attack. It also has multiple astromech units, each one capable of making emergency repairs.

DATA FILE

TYPE: Cruiser
MANUFACTURER: Theed Palace Space Vessel Engineering Corps
SPEED: 920 kph (572 mph)
MODEL: Modified J-Type 327 Nubian
LENGTH: 76 m (249 ft 4 in)
HYPERDRIVE: Class 1.8
WEAPONS: None

Forward station viewing windows

TRAVEL IN STYLE
This ship is exclusive to the royal family of Naboo. It includes quarters for the Queen and her handmaidens, equipped with climate-controlled wardrobes.

Sublight engine

Chromium hull can deflect laser attacks

Heroic Droids
During Queen Amidala's escape from the Trade Federation's blockade on Naboo, the royal starship's hyperdrive is damaged. Astromech droids are quickly deployed to the outer hull to repair it.

When the damaged ship needs new parts, it lands on Tatooine. It is here that Padmé Amidala first meets Anakin Skywalker.

NABOO ROYAL CRUISER

CUSTOM-BUILT J-TYPE DIPLOMATIC BARGE

DATA FILE

TYPE: Diplomatic barge
MANUFACTURER: Theed
Palace Space Vessel
Engineering Corps
SPEED: 2,000 kph
(1,243 mph)
MODEL: J-type
LENGTH: 39 m (128 ft)
HYPERDRIVE: Class 0.7
WEAPONS: None

THE INVASION OF NABOO convinces the peaceful planet to upgrade its diplomatic vessels. Though it still travels without weapons, this barge is far faster and better shielded than the J-type Nubian starship that came before it. It also boasts a range of backup systems in case of malfunctions or sabotage.

ROOM TO RELAX

The J-type diplomatic barge has spacious interiors designed for comfort. It has room for four prestigious passengers as well as up to five crew and six guards.

Cooling vents

Cockpit

Starboard thruster cover

Shiny chromium plating

Starboard sensor array cowling

Diplomatic Missions

During the Clone Wars, Senator Amidala travels by Naboo cruiser to meet with Duchess Satine Kryze on Mandalore. She also attends a refugee conference on Alderaan.

Senator Amidala travels in the Naboo cruiser to Coruscant, where she intends to vote against the Military Creation Act.

CSS-1 CORELLIAN STAR SHUTTLE

REPUBLIC SHUTTLE

BUILT FOR DIPLOMACY RATHER than battle, the CSS-1 shuttle has an impressive meeting room and comfortable quarters for VIP guests. It can carry up to 200 passengers, as well as enough supplies to last for three years. It is also equipped with an unusually strong deflector shield.

Heavily armored exterior

A pirate known as the Crimson Corsair captains a heavily modified CSS-1 named the *Meson Martinet*.

One of three ion engines

Narrow viewing windows for security

LOST SHIP

The Corellian Engineering Corporation designs an upgraded model—the CCS-8. Unfortunately, construction is put on hold indefinitely after the Clone Wars erupt.

Chancellor Transport

Shortly after his appointment to Supreme Chancellor of the Republic, Sheev Palpatine and the Jedi Council travel together to Naboo aboard the CSS-1 named the *Perpetuus*.

CRUCIBLE

YOUNGLING TRANSPORT

DATA FILE

TYPE: Corvette
MANUFACTURER: Rendili
Vehicle Corporation
MODEL: *Paladin*-class
corvette
LENGTH: 99 m (324 ft 10 in)
HYPERDRIVE: Class 2
WEAPONS: None

CUSTOM-BUILT FOR the Jedi in the time of the Old Republic, the *Crucible* has been in service for quite some time. It is used in the training of Jedi younglings, who learn how to construct their own lightsabers from kyber crystals while aboard.

When their chaperone Ahsoka Tano is kidnapped, six Jedi younglings land the *Crucible* on the planet Florrum and set out to rescue her.

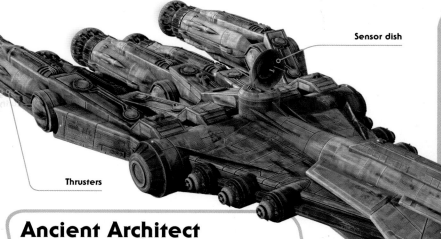

Sensor dish

Thrusters

LONG SERVICE

For many years, the *Crucible* takes younglings to the planet Ilum for an important Jedi ritual called The Gathering. The *Crucible* meets its end when it is shot down by Weequay pirates over the planet Florrum.

Ancient Architect

The ancient architect droid Professor Huyang serves on the *Crucible*. He has taught endless younglings how to build lightsabers, including Yoda.

Cockpit viewport

Docking hatch

LUXURY YACHT

PERSONAL LUXURY YACHT 3000

DATA FILE

TYPE: Luxury craft
MANUFACTURER: SoroSuub Corporation
SPEED: 850 kph (528 mph)
MODEL: SoroSuub 3000
LENGTH: 55.5 m (182 ft)
HYPERDRIVE: Class 2
WEAPONS: None

IN THE TIME OF THE Republic, diplomats use luxury yachts for meetings and travel. They become less popular during the chaos of the Clone Wars, when they are seen as easy targets for pirates and Separatists.

TRAVEL IN STYLE

Luxury yachts are common vehicles in wealthier systems. Built for comfort, they include a grand observation deck and a swimming pool, as well as five personal cabins for crew and guests.

Rear observation deck

Docking coupling

Bridge viewport

Comm tranceiver

Hyperdrive engine

Obi-Wan Kenobi briefly pilots a luxury yacht while disguised as a bounty hunter alongside Cad Bane and Moralo Eval.

Delivery Service

The pirate Hondo Ohnaka uses a luxury yacht named *Fortune and Glory* as a smuggling ship. He uses it to deliver weapons to Saw Gerrera on Onderon during the Clone Wars.

LIBERTINE

CUSTOM STAR YACHT

DATA FILE

TYPE: Custom Star Yacht
MANUFACTURER: Guild d'Lanseaux
MODEL: Unique craft
LENGTH: 52.92 m (173 ft 7 in)
HYPERDRIVE: Equipped
WEAPONS: None

THIS SLEEK SHIP is stylish, fast, and above all, luxurious. Although it is the property of a powerful businessman, that doesn't stop the criminal known as DJ taking it for himself. It makes the perfect escape ship when DJ, Rose, and Finn have to leave Canto Bight in a hurry.

Life of Luxury

The *Libertine*'s lavish interior is designed to impress. Its owner, Korfé Bennux-Ai, uses it to entertain guests and make business deals.

Cockpit

Expensive reflective hull coating

Recessed sublight engines

Forward repulsor projector plate

DJ, Rose, and Finn use the *Libertine* to infiltrate Snoke's Mega-Destroyer, the *Supremacy*.

FINDER'S FEE

DJ's lock-picking skills serve him well. After he boards the *Libertine*, none of its owner's private possessions stay private for very long!

TRADE FEDERATION LANDING SHIP

C-9979 LANDING CRAFT

DATA FILE

TYPE: Landing transport
MANUFACTURER: Haor Chall Engineering
SPEED: 587 kph (365 mph)
MODEL: C-9979
LENGTH: 210 m (689 ft)
HYPERDRIVE: None
WEAPONS: 2 laser cannons, 4 turret-mounted cannons

DON'T BE DECEIVED BY the elegant design of this troop transport. This computer-controlled vessel is packed with deadly battle droids, tanks, and even a mobile command center. Just one of these ships is enough to conquer a vulnerable world.

Wingtip laser cannon

Main sensor array

Multi-Troop Transport deployment doors

ALL ABOARD
One C-9979 can carry 11 Multi-Troop Transports and 361 additional battle droids. Its single "foot" enables it to land in densely forested and built-up areas, despite its enormous wingspan.

Destruction on Dathomir
General Grevious uses multiple C-9979s and their onboard armies to lay waste to the planet Dathomir and wipe out the Nightsisters coven that lives there.

Several C-9979s are deployed as part of the Trade Federation's unprovoked attack on the planet Naboo.

TECHNO UNION STARSHIP

HARDCELL-CLASS INTERSTELLAR TRANSPORT

Laser cannon

TECHNO UNION TRANSPORTS are a common sight before the Clone Wars, but are not used as military vehicles until the first Battle of Geonosis. With their conventional rocket propulsion and limited weaponry, they are vulnerable and largely ineffective against Galactic Republic forces.

ROCKET LAUNCHER
The starship's propulsion system relies on six large thrusters and retro rockets burning combustible fuel. With no repulsorlifts, it has limited maneuverability within a planetary atmosphere.

Titanium hull

Fuel lines

Rocket thruster

Fire to the Fuel
Anakin Skywalker realizes that the rocket fuel used by Hardcell transports is a major weakness on the battlefield. He orders his clone troopers to target their fuel cells—with explosive results.

Pressed into service at the start of the Clone Wars, the Techno Union starships are used to deploy IG-227 *Hailfire*-class droid tanks on the planet Geonosis.

Landing leg

175

SEPARATIST SUPPLY SHIP

HEMISPHERICAL HEAVY TRANSPORT

DATA FILE

TYPE: Transport
MANUFACTURER: Hoersh-
Kessel Drive Inc.
MODEL: DH-Omni
Support Vessel
WIDTH: 1,257 m (4,125 ft)
HYPERDRIVE: Class 6
WEAPONS: Point-defense
laser cannons

THIS VESSEL IS ONE of the biggest ships in the Separatist fleet, providing vital support for front-line forces in the Clone Wars. Its vast cargo bays can accommodate weapons, landing craft, battle droid troops, food for organic combatants, and more.

CARGO AND CREW

The ship is crewed by B1 battle droids and one T-series tactical droid. However, most of the droids aboard are inactive cargo, awaiting deployment on landing craft.

Command tower

Docking channel

Dooku Defender

Supply ships are rarely used for front-line duties. However, at least five supply ships take part in the Separatist defense of Serreno, which is designed to protect Count Dooku's home planet.

Armored hull

Separatist insignia

Three clone troopers use stolen Umbaran fighters to sabotage a supply ship from the inside.

ACCLAMATOR-CLASS ASSAULT SHIP

TRANSGALACTIC MILITARY TRANSPORT SHIP

DATA FILE

TYPE: Assault ship
MANUFACTURER: Rothana Heavy Engineering
SPEED: 1,200 kph (745 mph)
MODEL: *Acclamator*-class
LENGTH: 752 m (2,467 ft 2 in)
HYPERDRIVE: Equipped
WEAPONS: 12 quad laser turrets, 24 laser cannons, 4 missile launchers

THESE ASSAULT SHIPS ARE a predecessor of the later Star Destroyers. They are built for the Clone Wars, under false orders supposedly issued by the Jedi Council. This is all part of Darth Sidious's evil plan to take over the galaxy.

During the Clone Wars, *Acclamator*-class ships are stationed at Coruscant, ready to carry clone troopers across the galaxy.

Command tower

Twin hyperdrive engines

Republic colors

HEAVY LOAD

Each *Acclamator*-class assault ship requires a crew of 700 and can carry up to 16,000 clone troopers.

Ground Fall

Unlike many craft of this size, *Acclamator*-class assault ships can land on planets, where they deploy Republic forces in an effort to retake the worlds from Separatist control.

Four missile launchers

Quad laser turret

REBEL TRANSPORT

GR-75 MEDIUM TRANSPORT

DATA FILE

TYPE: Transport
MANUFACTURER:
Gallofree Yards, Inc.
SPEED: 650 kph (403 mph)
MODEL: GR-75
LENGTH: 90 m (295 ft 3 in)
HYPERDRIVE: Class 4
WEAPONS: 4 twin
laser cannons

NEVER IN THE SAME place for long, this cargo transporter becomes a potent symbol of the Rebel Alliance. Its organic-looking hull can deflect Imperial sensors, making it ideal for stealthy supply runs. Though rarely used in combat, some GR-75's are retrofitted for battle.

CARGO CARRIER

A GR-75 can accommodate 19,000 metric tons (41,887,830 lbs) of cargo. The modular cargo pods are held in place by a magnetic shield.

Command bridge

Secondary engines

Primary engines

Cargo modules

Clamshell hull

The rebels use GR-75s to flee the ice planet Hoth when the Empire locates their secret base.

Death Star Strike

In addition to fighting in the Battle of Scarif, several GR-75s take part in the Battle of Endor. They support the rebels' larger battlecruisers as they launch their attack on the Death Star II.

ATMOSPHERIC ASSAULT LANDER

DATA FILE

TYPE: Troop Transport
MANUFACTURER: Sienar-Jaemus Army Systems
SPEED: 900 kph (559 mph)
MODEL: AAL-1971/9.1
LENGTH: 17.8 m (58 ft 4 in)
WEAPONS: 1 antipersonnel blaster cannon

IN BATTLE, SPEED IS everything. These clunky-looking troop transports can deliver 20 battle-ready soldiers from an orbiting station to landfall in less than thirty seconds. This ensures that the best and brightest of the First Order are ready to blaze into combat without delay.

BATTLE READY

An AAL is operated by a single pilot. Each transport can carry two squadrons of stormtroopers into the First Order's many dangerous battles and missions.

Elevated cockpit for standing pilot

Rotating gun turret and gunner's hatch

Boarding ramp in raised position

Terrain sensors

Sturdy landing gear

Overkill

Four AALs are used during the assault on the helpless inhabitants of Tuanul. This attack leads to the capture of Poe Dameron.

AALs are part of the First Order fleet that lands on Takodana. They deploy stormtroopers to Maz Kanata's castle.

DATA FILE

TYPE: Transport
MANUFACTURER: Custom
SPEED: 750 kph (466 mph)
MODEL: SS-54 Assault Ship
WIDTH: 16.18 m (53 ft 1 in)
HYPERDRIVE: Class 1
WEAPONS: 1 heavy laser cannon

COBBLED TOGETHER FROM PARTS left over from the Galactic Civil War, the Resistance Transport is a surprisingly functional vehicle. Used by the Resistance to deploy troops into battle against the First Order, it is both tough and versatile.

Finn and Rose use the cockpit module of a Resistance Transport to reach Canto Bight.

Stabilizer fin with static discharge vanes

Hull shell made from surplus plating

Heavy laser cannon

Transport pod built from Mark 2 B-wing cockpit

Boarding area leading to troop compartment

To the Rescue

Leia commands a squadron of Resistance fighters aboard a Resistance Transport during the skirmish on Takodana.

REUSED PARTS

Resistance transports are typically designed to carry 20 troops. They require only a single pilot, who controls the ship from a detachable cockpit made from recycled B-wing components.

SEPARATIST FRIGATE

MUNIFICENT-CLASS STAR FRIGATE

DATA FILE

TYPE: Frigate
MANUFACTURER:
Hoersch-Kessel Drive Inc.
SPEED: 950 kph (590 mph)
MODEL: *Munificent*-class
LENGTH: 825 m (2,707 ft)
HYPERDRIVE: Class 1
WEAPONS: 2 heavy
turbolaser cannons,
2 long-range heavy
ion cannons, 38 point-
defense cannons, 26
twin turbolaser cannons,
20 light turbolaser
turrets, 8 flak guns,
hyperwave jammer

GROSSLY OVERPOWERED
for its size, this battle-ready
frigate is commissioned by
the InterGalactic Banking
Clan to assist the Separatist
cause. It is capable of carrying
150,000 battle droids, and
just one frigate can
overwhelm an entire planet.

ALL ABOARD
It takes a crew of
200 to operate one
Separatist star frigate.
Only a handful serve
in the command
tower, which rises
up from the front
of the vessel.

Long-range hyperwave
transceiver mast

Command
tower

Separatist
insignia

Sensor tower

Separatist frigates
attack Republic ships
as part of an attempt
to seize a valuable
Jedi Holocron.

Trouble over Toydaria
Yoda's ship is shot down by two *Munificent*-class
frigates over the planet Toydaria in a Separatist
plot to disrupt diplomatic relations.

REPUBLIC FRIGATE

CONSULAR-CLASS CRUISER

DATA FILE

TYPE: Space cruiser
MANUFACTURER: Corellian Engineering Corporation
SPEED: 1,200 kph (745 mph)
MODEL: *Consular*-class
LENGTH: 139 m (456 ft)
HYPERDRIVE: Class 2
WEAPONS: Retrofitted with 5 twin turbolaser turrets and 1 twin laser cannon

USED BY THE JEDI and the Galactic Senate on diplomatic missions before the Clone Wars, these cruisers are retrofitted as combat frigates when war breaks out. Their upgrades include armored hull plating and laser cannon batteries.

Jedi representatives travel to Naboo in a *Consular*-class cruiser, intending to mediate a trade dispute.

GREAT LENGTHS

Republic cruisers that have undergone the Charger c70 retrofit for use in the Clone Wars are longer than those that have not.

Communications and sensor dish

Sublight engines

Twin turbolaser cannon turret

Docking ring

Twin laser cannon

Into the Fire

A *Consular*-class cruiser docks with a battle-damaged Republic flagship that is burning up. The cruiser is the only escape for Anakin Skywalker, Ahsoka Tano, and Aayla Secura!

Detachable salon pod for diplomatic meetings

Navigational sensor dish

PELTA-CLASS FRIGATE

REPUBLIC MEDICAL FRIGATE

DATA FILE

TYPE: Medical frigate
MANUFACTURER: Kuat Drive Yards
SPEED: 800 kph (497 mph)
MODEL: YT-2400
LENGTH: 282 m (925 ft 2 in)
HYPERDRIVE: Class 2
WEAPONS: Point-defense laser cannons

DURING THE CLONE Wars, the *Pelta*-class frigate is a common sight at the edges of space battles. It is used by the Republic Navy to treat injured clone soldiers. The more honorable generals in the Separatist fleet usually don't attack it.

During the Imperial era, a modified Pelta frigate named *Phoenix Home* serves as a rebel cell's capital ship, until it is destroyed by Darth Vader.

Command tower

Heavily armored external layer

Folding wings

Shuttle docking station

Point-defense light laser cannon

FRIGATE EQUIPMENT
Each *Pelta*-class frigate can carry up to 900 crew, and is equipped with 16 escape pods. *Phoenix Home* is modified to include turbo laser batteries.

No Mercy
The Separatists target many of these frigates during the *Malevolence* campaign. The ships are ruthlessly cut down by vicious General Grievous.

STEALTH SHIP

CORVETTE WITH A CLOAK

THE REPUBLIC'S STEALTH SHIP is able to turn invisible. It is designed with an experimental cloaking device, which allows it to sneak past Separatist blockades. As well as being impossible to see when cloaked, it is undetectable by scanners and sensors.

DATA FILE

TYPE: Corvette
MANUFACTURER: Sienar Design Systems
SPEED: 950 kph (590 mph)
MODEL: Prototype
LENGTH: 99.7 m (327 ft)
HYPERDRIVE: None
WEAPONS: Laser cannons, proton torpedo launchers

FLARE FOR SURVIVAL
The stealth ship cannot fire its laser cannons or proton torpedoes while cloaked, but it can launch flares to confuse enemy tracking torpedoes.

One of 28 cloak projectors

Modular hull

Laser cannon

Sensor rectenna

On a mission to the planet Christophsis, Anakin Skywalker uses the stealth ship to attack a blockade, rather than sneak through it.

Trick of the Light
The only sign of the cloaked stealth ship is a small amount of light distortion when it moves through space. This is clearest when it passes in front of a planet or moon.

Cockpit viewport

ACUSHNET

PIRATE FRIGATE

ORIGINALLY INTENDED AS DROID ships for the Separatists, the *Corona*-class armed frigates were deemed unsuitable and their production abruptly halted. Most of the line is sold to investors and ship collectors. The notorious pirate Hondo Ohnaka steals one, named *Acushnet*, and declares it his flagship.

Central launch hatch

SHIPS AND TANKS

The *Acushnet* carries six *Flarestar*-class ships and 12 speeder tanks, and requires a crew of 64. The ship has eight retractable landing legs, and one of them also functions as a boarding ramp.

Laser cannon

Shipwrecked

When Count Dooku's ship crashes on the planet Vanqor, he encounters Hondo and his pirate gang. Their massive saucer-shaped ship is parked over the debris of Dooku's ruined transport.

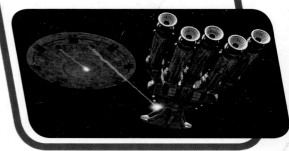

While on a training trip with younglings, Ahsoka Tano is forced to defend their ship from an attack by the *Acushnet*.

IMPERIAL INTERDICTOR

EXPERIMENTAL CRUISER

DATA FILE

TYPE: Cruiser
MANUFACTURER: Sienar
Fleet Systems
SPEED: 975 kph (605 mph)
MODEL: Protoype
LENGTH: 1,129 m (3,074 ft
1 in)
HYPERDRIVE: Class 2
WEAPONS: 20 quad laser
cannons

IN AN EFFORT TO STOP enemy ships from escaping past planetary blockades, the Imperials come up with a new strategy using an experimental ship—the Interdictor. This ship generates a powerful gravity well that can stop the hyperdrive units of nearby craft.

Imperfected

While trying to catch a rebel ship, the experimental cruiser accidentally captures its own escort craft. The two ships then collide, and the Interdictor prototype is destroyed in the explosion!

Command
bridge

Gravity well
projector

Laser cannon
targeting system

The Interdictor is under the command of Admiral Brom Titus. This arrogant Imperial is very proud of of his ship.

FULLY LOADED

The Imperial Interdictor is an intimidating ship. Huge gravity well projectors impede hyperspace drives. It carries 24 TIE fighters and has more than 2,800 crew.

IMPERIAL LIGHT CARRIER

QUASAR FIRE-CLASS CRUISER-CARRIER

DATA FILE

TYPE: Carrier
MANUFACTURER: SoroSuub
Corporation
SPEED: 250 kph (155 mph)
MODEL: *Quasar Fire*-class
LENGTH: 340 m (1,115 ft
6 in)
HYPERDRIVE: Class 2
WEAPONS: 2 light
turbolaser batteries

THIS HUGE STARSHIP SERVES as a mobile base for enforcing Imperial law. Stationed in orbit of occupied worlds, its wide hangar deck allows multiple TIE fighters to launch simultaneously. This makes it an effective alternative to the even larger Star Destroyer.

Bridge

A PHOENIX RISES

An Imperial light carrier stolen by the rebels becomes the second ship to bear the name *Phoenix Home*. It is repainted in rebel colors and used as a base for the A-wing starfighters of Phoenix Squadron.

Main thruster strip

Launch bay

Battle Bays

The carrier's wide hangar deck is divided into four large bays. During the Battle of Atollon, the rebels deploy recently acquired Y-wing fighters from the bays of their stolen Imperial ship.

Cham Syndulla and his daughter Hera concoct a daring plan to steal an Imperial light carrier for the rebellion.

TANTIVE IV

REBEL BLOCKADE RUNNER

DATA FILE

TYPE: Corvette
MANUFACTURER: Corellian
Engineering Corporation
SPEED: 950 kph (590 mph)
MODEL: CR90 Corvette
LENGTH: 150 m (495 ft 2 in)
HYPERDRIVE: Class 2
WEAPONS: Single laser
cannon, 2 twin turbolasers

THE *TANTIVE IV*
belongs to the Royal
House of Alderaan.
Princess Leia and her
adoptive father, Bail
Organa, use this state
ship for both diplomatic
missions for the Empire
and secret missions for
the Rebellion.

When Darth Vader captures
the *Tantive IV*, Leia hides the
Death Star plans inside R2-D2.

Ion turbine
drive block

12-passenger
capacity
escape pod

VIP VESSEL

Up to 46 crew and 39 diplomats are
stationed on the *Tantive IV*. The ship
contains dining rooms, conference halls,
and escape pods for quick exits.

Airlock

Twin turbolaser
turret

Just in Time

The *Tantive IV* plays a key role in
capturing the Death Star plans. It
escapes from the Battle of Scarif—and
Darth Vader—with seconds to spare!

Lower twin
turbolaser

Docking hatch

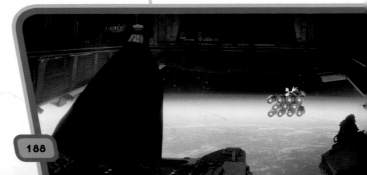

REBEL CORVETTE

THE *SPHYRNA*-CLASS CORVETTE is more commonly known as a Hammerhead corvette due to its striking and unusual prow design. Adaptable and reliable ships, many Hammerheads join the rebel fleet.

DATA FILE

TYPE: Corvette
MANUFACTURER: Corellian Engineering Corporation
SPEED: 900 kph (559 mph)
MODEL: *Sphyrna*-class "Hammerhead" corvette
LENGTH: 315 m (1,033 ft 5 in)
HYPERDRIVE: Equipped
WEAPONS: 3 dual laser cannons

The young Princess Leia delivers three Hammerhead corvettes to rebels on the planet Lothal.

Command bridge

Dual laser cannon

Add-on starboard module

Escape pods

Forward landing gear

Hammer Blow

A Hammerhead corvette is vital to the rebels' victory in the Battle of Scarif. Admiral Raddus orders its pilots to ram an Imperial Star Destroyer.

UPGRADED

By the Battle of Scarif, many Hammerheads are upgraded to include an extra sublight engine and two add-on modules.

REBEL CRUISER

EF76 NEBULON-B ESCORT FRIGATE

DATA FILE

TYPE: Escort Frigate
MANUFACTURER: Kuat Drive Yards
SPEED: 1,200 kph (745 mph)
MODEL: EF76 Nebulon-B
LENGTH: 300 m (984 ft 3 in)
HYPERDRIVE: Class 2
WEAPONS: 12 laser cannons, 12 turbolasers

THE NEBULON-B IS A versatile ship that can be adapted to different roles in the rebel fleet. Rebels outfit some cruisers to provide medical assistance, equipping others for search-and-rescue tasks, combat missions, or scouting operations.

To Battle

In an effort to take down the second Death Star, a rebel cruiser flies into battle alongside the other rebel warships and fighters, drawing heavy enemy fire.

Long-range communications array

Main medical bay areas can hold 700 patients

Deflector shield generator

Docking tubes

Propulsion module houses seven ion engines

Bridge and command deck

SMALLER CRAFT

A Nebulon-B can act as a ship carrier. Its hangar can house a squadron of fighters and several shuttles, all ready for battle.

After Luke Skywalker loses his hand in battle, he is outfitted with a mechanical hand aboard *Redemption*, a medical cruiser.

TRADE FEDERATION BATTLESHIP

COMBAT-ENABLED CARGO FREIGHTER

DATA FILE

TYPE: Battleship
MANUFACTURER:
Hoersch-Kessel Drive, Inc.
SPEED: 500 kph (310 mph)
MODEL: Modified *Lucrehulk-*class LH-3210 cargo freighter
LENGTH: 3,170 m (10,400 ft)
HYPERDRIVE: Class 2
WEAPONS: 185 quad laser batteries, 520 assault laser cannons, 51 turbolasers

AS WAR AGAINST THE Republic looms, the Trade Federation's freighters are secretly modified into battleships. However, the conversion is not perfect, and the installed turbolasers do not cover every angle, leaving blind spots that can be targeted by enemy ships.

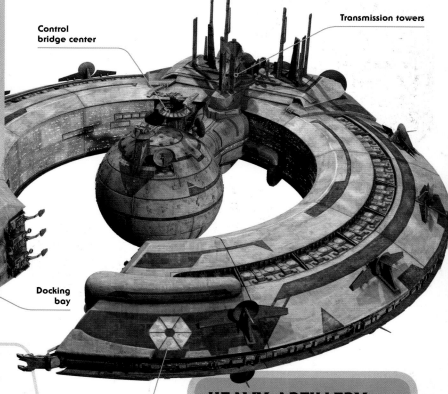

Transmission towers

Control bridge center

Droid signal receiver

Docking bay

Separatist logo

Naboo Invasion

The Trade Federation battleships play a key role in the Invasion of Naboo. A droid-controlling Lucrehulk, the *Vuutun Palaa*, is at the heart of the blockade.

HEAVY ARTILLERY

These massive battleships are able to hold 1,500 vulture droid starfighters; 50 C-9979 landing craft; 6,250 armored assault tanks; and more than 329,000 B1 battle droids

MALEVOLENCE

SUBJUGATOR-CLASS HEAVY CRUISER

DURING THE CLONE WARS, General Grievous's huge flagship leaves death and devastation in its wake. Its massive ion cannons disrupt the control systems of surrounding ships, disabling their energy weapons and deflector shields.

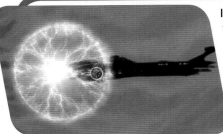

In its first engagement, the *Malevolence* uses its ion cannon on three Republic attack cruisers. Just one blast renders the ships helpless, and they are destroyed.

Weapons batteries

Sensor array

Command tower

Point-defense laser cannon

Port ion cannon

GREAT LENGTHS

Four times longer than a *Venator*-class Star Destroyer, the *Malevolence* has an internal shuttle train system to deploy supplies and troops and is crewed by 900 battle droids.

Going Down

The *Malevolence* meets its end when the Jedi Anakin Skywalker sabotages its navigation systems. This causes it to plunge headlong into the Dead Moon of Antar.

INVISIBLE HAND

PROVIDENCE-CLASS DREADNOUGHT

COMMANDED BY GENERAL GRIEVOUS, the *Invisible Hand* plays a key role in the last great battle of the Clone Wars. With the sinister Sith Lord Count Dooku holding Chancellor Palpatine prisoner aboard the failing ship, the Jedi Order must rush to the rescue.

Two-man Mission
In their fight to save the Chancellor, Anakin Skywalker and Obi-Wan Kenobi battle their way through the *Invisible Hand* to the tower where Count Dooku awaits.

Main upper
sensor tower

Secondary, ventral sensor pod

The *Invisible Hand* is controlled with a droid brain. This means that Anakin Skywalker can override controls and fly the ship. It's still a bumpy landing!

STRONG DEFENSE
The *Invisible Hand* is a difficult ship to attack. There are 20 squadrons of droid starfighters ready to defend it. Count Dooku turns the ship's upper sensor tower into his lair, calling it the "Wizard's Tower."

REPUBLIC ATTACK CRUISER

STAR DESTROYER

THE WAR BETWEEN THE REPUBLIC and the Separatists leads to a demand for larger and more powerful battleships. The Republic Navy expands to include the Republic attack cruisers, massive warships often referred to as "Star Destroyers."

DATA FILE

TYPE: Star Destroyer
MANUFACTURER: Kuat Drive Yards
SPEED: 975 kph (606 mph)
MODEL: *Venator*-class Star Destroyer
LENGTH: 1,137 m (3,730 ft 3 in)
HYPERDRIVE: Class 1
WEAPONS: 8 heavy turbolasers, 2 medium dual turbolaser cannons, 52 point-defense laser cannons, 6 tractor beam projectors, torpedoes

FULLY EQUIPPED
Venator-class Star Destroyers can carry more than 420 starfighters (including V-wings, Z-95 Headhunters, and Jedi starfighters); 40 LAAT/i gunships; and 24 AT-TEs.

Command bridge

Sliding flight deck cover

Crewed areas

Docking port

Separatist leader Nute Gunray is held captive aboard a Republic attack cruiser, until Asajj Ventress frees him from his cell.

Coruscant Defenders
During the Battle of Coruscant, more than 1,000 Republic attack cruisers are deployed in defense of the planet.

CORONET

PERSONAL SPACELINER

Elegant halls
on upper decks

Officer rooms

Command bridge

THE *CORONET* IS DUCHESS

Satine Kryze of Mandalore's
personal luxury spaceliner.
This one-of-a-kind ship is
practically a spacefaring
palace. It serves as a
testament to the
engineering and wealth
of the Mandalorians.

Obi-Wan Kenobi defends
Duchess Satine and the *Coronet*
from the extremist group known
as Death Watch.

Assassin Infiltration

Duchess Satine and her retinue travel in the *Coronet*
to Coruscant for an important diplomatic mission.
Unfortunately, the spaceliner is infiltrated with
Separatist-controlled assassin probe droids.

SHIP NUMBERS

The lower decks of the
Coronet are used for
cargo transport. The
ship requires a crew
of 75, and has eight
engines all working
in unison.

Laser and
Ion cannons

IMPERIAL STAR DESTROYER

CAPITAL WARSHIP

THE EMPIRE USES THE immense size of its military to intimidate its enemies. This makes the Imperial Star Destroyers a huge success. Heavily armed, densely shielded, and equipped with a full-scale army, one Star Destroyer is powerful enough to conquer a world.

Command bridge

Flight control

Turbolaser turret

Pursuit tractor beams

Weapon-targeting systems

BIG NUMBERS

The Empire has thousands of Star Destroyers. Each ship carries a minimum of 72 TIE fighters; 20 AT-ATs; 30 AT-STs; 8 *Lambda*-class Imperial shuttles; 9,700 stormtroopers; 9,200 officers; and 27,850 enlisted crew.

Close Call

The *Millennium Falcon* weaves so closely between two Star Destroyers that they almost collide while trying to catch it.

Star Destroyers are often used to deter rebel activity on troublesome planets.

EXECUTOR

SITH LORD FLAGSHIP

DATA FILE

TYPE: Super Star Destroyer
MANUFACTURER: Kuat Drive Yards
SPEED: 100 kph (62 mph)
MODEL: *Executor*-class Star Dreadnaught
LENGTH: 19,000 m (62,335 ft 10 in)
HYPERDRIVE: Class 1
WEAPONS: Over 5,000 turbolasers and ion cannons

SEVERAL SHIPS HAVE BORNE the title "Super Star Destroyer." This term applies to any ship larger than the Imperial Star Destroyers. The biggest of these is the *Executor*, the personal flagship of the Sith Lord Darth Vader.

FULL CAPACITY

An *Executor*-class Star Dreadnaught carries more than 1,000 ships, and the craft has thousands of crew. A twin to the *Executor*, the *Eclipse*, serves as the Emperor's flagship.

Command tower

Central space housing more than 5,000 turbolasers and ion cannons

13 thruster engines on underside

During the Battle of Endor, the gravity well of the second Death Star pulls the *Executor* in, destroying it instantly.

Titanium-reinforced hull

Replacement

The first commander of the *Executor* is Admiral Kendal Ozzel. Darth Vader executes him after his mistakes at the Battle of Hoth allow many rebels to escape. Ozzel is replaced by Admiral Firmus Piett, whose performance has impressed Vader.

PROFUNDITY

MC75 MODIFIED STAR CRUISER

DATA FILE

TYPE: Star cruiser
MANUFACTURER: Mon Calamari Ship Yards
SPEED: 650 kph (404 mph)
MODEL: MC75
LENGTH: 1,204 m (3,950 ft)
HYPERDRIVE: Class 1
WEAPONS: 20 point-defense laser cannons, 12 turbolaser cannons, 4 ion cannons, 6 tractor beam projectors, 12 proton torpedo launchers

MON CALAMARI MC75 cruisers are repurposed from buildings and exploration ships, and require a 3,225-strong crew. These massive craft are a valuable addition to the rebel fleet. One ship that truly proves itself in the fight against the Empire is the *Profundity*, which is commanded by the highly experienced Admiral Raddus.

LOW BRIDGE

The *Profundity*'s bridge is built on the underside of the ship. This is very useful in battle, as it gives the crew a clear view of their immediate surrounds and of Scarif's planetary shield system.

Dorsal communications transmission mast

Aft deflector shield emitter ray

Ordnance pod

Battle of Scarif

During the Battle of Scarif, all manner of rebel ships fight together against the might of the Empire. The *Profundity* plays its part in gaining a major victory for the Rebel Alliance.

Command bridge

Aboard the *Profundity*, Admiral Raddus waits to receive the Death Star plans from Rogue One leader Jyn Erso.

HOME ONE

MC80A STAR CRUISER

DATA FILE

TYPE: Star cruiser
MANUFACTURER: Mon Calamari Ship Yards
SPEED: 975 kph (606 mph)
MODEL: MC80A
LENGTH: 1,300 m (4,265 ft)
HYPERDRIVE: Class 1
WEAPONS: 29 turbolaser batteries, 36 ion cannon batteries, 6 tractor beam projectors

THE MC80A STAR CRUISERS are originally intended for long missions in deep space. These civilian vessels are refitted by the Mon Calamari for battle after the Empire attempts to conquer their world. *Home One*, also known as the Headquarters Frigate, serves as the Rebel Alliance's answer to the Empire's Star Destroyers.

ADAPTED HOME

Sections of *Home One* are filled with water, replicating the Mon Calamari's natural environment. The ship's holographic amphitheater has been repurposed into a briefing room for the Rebel Alliance.

Home One's captain, Admiral Ackbar, leads the rebel forces into battle against the Death Star II.

Main shuttle

Hangar entrance

Ion engine

Mon Calamari Assault

Along with the *Home One*, other MC80s such as the *Independence* and the *Defiance*, join the rebel assault on the Empire's second Death Star.

RADDUS

RESISTANCE FLAGSHIP

DATA FILE

TYPE: Star Cruiser
MANUFACTURER: Mon Calamari Shipyards/Corellian Engineering Corporation
MODEL: MC85
HYPERDRIVE: Equipped
LENGTH: 3,438.37 m (11,280 ft 9 in)
WEAPONS: Heavy turbolasers, heavy ion cannons, point-defense laser turrets, proton torpedo launchers

A MIGHTY HEAVY CRUISER that once served in the New Republic fleet, the *Raddus* has since become the flagship of the Resistance. General Leia Organa uses the *Raddus* as her headquarters after the Resistance evacuates its base on the planet D'Qar.

A First Order attack on the *Raddus'* hangar causes a huge explosion. Many Resistance starfighters are destroyed, and Poe and BB-8 only just escape.

SHIP SHAPE

The *Raddus* was built by Mon Calamari engineers. Its design is similar to the MC80 Mon Calamari cruisers that served in the rebel fleet during the Galactic Civil War.

Turbolaser blister

Primary bridge

Main sublight engines

Internal main hangar bay

In Command

For a short while, the bridge of the *Raddus* becomes the new nerve center of the Resistance. But soon afterward, a First Order attack blasts the bridge into ruins, and badly wounds General Leia Organa.

FINALIZER

RESURGENT-CLASS STAR DESTROYER

THE *FINALIZER* IS BUILT in secret by the First Order, violating treaties meant to bring peace to the galaxy. Admirers of the former Empire welcome it as a return to the glory days of order through strength.

Finn serves on the *Finalizer* as stormtrooper FN-2187 before deserting with the Resistance fighter Poe Dameron.

Bridge deflector shield projector

Command bridge

Flight deck deflector shield projector

Heavy turbolaser turret

Dark View

Kylo Ren watches from the bridge of the *Finalizer* as Starkiller Base fires its superweapon. In an instant, entire worlds are condemned to destruction.

REN'S DEN

The *Finalizer* is Kylo Ren's base of operations. He launches an attack on the planet Jakku from the ship.

SUPREMACY

FIRST ORDER HEADQUARTERS

DATA FILE

TYPE: Star Dreadnought
MANUFACTURER: Kuat-Entralla Engineering
MODEL: *Mega*-class
WIDTH: 60,542.68 m
(198,630 ft 10 in)
HYPERDRIVE: Equipped
WEAPONS: Thousands of heavy turbolasers and ion cannons, missile batteries

THE ONLY *MEGA*-CLASS STAR DESTROYER in the galaxy, this enormous vessel is Supreme Leader Snoke's flagship, and the heart of the First Order fleet. Inside its vast hull, legions of stormtroopers prepare for battle, and factories churn out advanced weapons and vehicles.

Snoke's throne room lies in the center of the ship. Here, Snoke watches events unfold from a raised throne, surrounded by his silent armored protectors, the Praetorian Guard.

Overbridge

Star Destroyer docking bays

Nerve Center

At the highest point of the ship, a huge tower looms over the city-like structures below. This is the overbridge—the entire ship is controlled from inside.

Main habitation decks

Heavy turbolaser towers

Invasion Force

The *Supremacy*'s enormous hangar bays are full of armored walkers, troop transports, and giant siege weapons, ready to conquer new worlds for the First Order.

IMPERIAL CONSTRUCTION MODULE

MANUFACTURING SPHERE

DATA FILE

TYPE: Space Station
MANUFACTURER: Huppla Pasa Tisc Shipwrights Collective
SPEED: 100 kph (62 mph)
MODEL: ICM-092792
DIAMETER: 828 m (2,716 ft 6 in)
HYPERDRIVE: None
WEAPONS: Point-defense system

DESIGNED BY THE GEONOSIANS, the Imperial construction module features state-of-the-art machinery for building and maintaining ships. Each construction sphere is capable of quickly producing a small fleet for the Empire.

Transmitter sends updates on progress

TOP SPEED

Each construction module is staffed by just three control technicians and 24 mechanics, but it can service more than 100 starfighters at a time. The main hangar can hold two starships and one shuttle.

Crane arm

Large cargo bay

Gas tanks holding project materials

Star Power

Several of these spherical building modules are used in the construction of the first Death Star. They are left orbiting Geonosis, abandoned as bait by Imperial agents hoping to snare curious rebels.

In a rebel attack against the Empire, Ezra Bridger orders an assault on one of the construction modules.

DEATH STAR

DS-1 ORBITAL BATTLE STATION

BUILT IN SECRET OVER 20 years, the Death Star is the Empire's most devastating weapon. Rumors of its power are expected to crush any hint of opposition to Imperial rule. Instead, news of the moon-sized battle station succeeds in spurring pockets of resistance across the galaxy to come together in an organized rebellion.

DATA FILE

TYPE: Battle station
MANUFACTURER: Advanced Weapons Research
MODEL: DS-1
DIAMETER: 160 km (99 mi)
HYPERDRIVE: Class 4
WEAPONS: Superlaser, 15,000 turbolasers, 2,500 ion cannons, 2,500 laser cannons, 768 tractor-beam emplacements

ROUND NUMBERS

More than one million Imperial personnel can serve on board the Death Star at any time. This includes almost 26,000 stormtroopers and the station commander, Wilhuff Tarkin.

Superlaser focus lens

Trash Trap

Luke Skywalker, Han Solo, and Chewbacca save Princess Leia from a cell on the Death Star—only for all four of them to end up trapped in the station's garbage compactor!

Equatorial trench

Quadanium steel hull

Galen Erso, the reluctant designer of the Death Star's superlaser, lets the rebels know the battle station has a weakness.

204

DEATH STAR II

UNFINISHED BUT FULLY OPERATIONAL BATTLE STATION

DATA FILE

TYPE: Battle station
MANUFACTURER: Advanced
Weapons Research
DIAMETER: 200 km
(124 mi)
HYPERDRIVE: Incomplete
WEAPONS: Superlaser,
30,000 turbolasers,
7,500 laser cannons,
5,000 ion cannons,
768 tractor beam
emplacements

THE SECOND BATTLE STATION to be known as
the Death Star is bigger and less vulnerable than
the first. It is still under construction in orbit of the
forest moon of Endor when it is attacked by the
Rebel Alliance, but it is far from defenseless. Its
planet-destroying superlaser is in full working order!

Emperor's Tower

SHIELDS UP

The incomplete Death
Star II is protected by
a powerful deflector
shield, beamed into
space from a
generator on
the moon of
Endor below.

Superlaser
focus lens

Surface
city
blocks

Equatorial
trench

When the seemingly dormant
Death Star engages its weapons,
the attacking rebel fleet realizes
it has been lured into a trap.

Exposed
superstructure

Rebel Uproar

Once the rebels learn the location of the second
Death Star, they plan a full assault. They hope to
destroy it while it is still under construction.

INDEX

74-Z speeder bike **36**
614-AvA speeder bike **36**

A
A-wing starfighter **112**
AA-9 Coruscant freighter **160**
AAL (Atmospheric Assault Lander) **179**
AAT battle tank **47**
Acclamator-class assault ship **177**
Acushnet **185**
Aka'jor-class shuttle **135**
Alpha-3 *Nimbus*-class V-wing starfighter **99**
Amidala, Padmé, H-type Nubian yacht **122**
Anakin's podracer **26**
ARC-170 starfighter **100**
Armored Assault Tank **47**
AT-ACT (All Terrain Armored Cargo Transport) **65**
AT-AT (All Terrain Armored Transport) **64**
AT-DP (All Terrain Defense Pod) **62**
AT-M6 (All Terrain MegaCaliber 6) **66**
AT-OT (All Terrain Open Transport) **60**
AT-RT (All Terrain Recon Transport) **61**
AT-ST (All Terrain Scout Transport) **63**
AT-TE (All Terrain Tactical Enforcer) **59**
Aurore-class freighter **161**

B
B-wing starfighters 113, **114**
Baktoid Armor Workshop 15, 46, 47, 49, 56, 57, 104
Baleen-class heavy freighter 167
Balutar-class swoop **33**
Bane, Cad, *Xanadu Blood* **104**
Bantha-II cargo skiff **55**
BARC (Biker Advanced Recon Commando) speeder **30**
Belbullab-22 starfighter **94**
Black One **120**
Blade Wing **113**
Bloodfin 28, **124**
Bongo submarine **79**
Botajef freighter-liner **160**
Braha'tok-class gunship **157**
Broken Horn **166**
Buirk'alor-class speeder **42**

C
C-9979 landing craft **174**
C-ROC *Gozanti*-class cruiser **166**
Canto Bight police speeder **44**
CK-6 swoop bike **31**
Class 4 container transport **165**
Clone swamp speeder **41**
Clone turbo tank **71**
Cloud car **21**
ComfortRide passenger airspeeder **10**
Consular-class cruiser **182**
Corellian Engineering Corporation 138, 147, 149, 153, 155, 156, 161, 163, 164, 167, 170, 182, 188
Corellian G9 rigger freighter **147**
Corellian star shuttle **170**
Corona-class frigate **185**
Coronet **195**
Corporate Alliance tank droid **69**
Coruscant, Battle of 11, 12, 95, 97, 100, 194
Coruscant air taxi **10**
Coruscant fire supression ship **12**
Coruscant freighter **160**
Coruscant police speeder **13**
Crucible **171**
CSS-1 Corellian star shuttle **170**

D
D-11 Naboo water speeder **77**
DDT (Defoliator Deployment Tank) **48**
Death Star 117, 188, 198, 203, **204**
Death Star II 107, 116, 178, 190, 197, 198, **205**
Delta-7 light interceptor **96**
Delta-class T-3c shuttle **141**
Desert skiff **55**
DH-Omni Support Vessel **176**
Dooku, Count
  Flitknot speeder **29**
  Invisible Hand **193**
  solar sailer **127**
Dornean gunship **157**
Droch-class boarding ship **87**
Droid tanks 68, **69**
Droid tri-fighter **95**
DSD1 dwarf spider droid **57**

E
Endor, Battle of 63, 114, 178, 197
Eravana **167**
Escape pods **86**
ETA-2 light interceptor 97, 99

ETA-class shuttle **131**
Executor 112, **197**

F
Fanblade fighter **93**
Fang fighter **103**
FC-20 speeder bike 28, **124**
Fett, Jango, *Slave I* **146**
Finalizer **201**
First Order shuttle **145**
First Order transporter **179**
Flarestar-class attack shuttle **136**
Flitknot speeder **29**
Freeco bike **31**

G
G9 *Rigger*-class freighter **147**
Gauntlet starfighter **102**
Geonosian starfighter **92**
Geonosis
  first Battle of 29, 56, 92, 125, 127, 175
  second Battle of 92
Ghost 88, 110, 111, 137, 138, 153
Gian speeder **40**
Ginivex-class fanblade starfighter **93**
Gondola speeder **76**
Gozanti-class cruiser **163**
GR-75 medium transport **178**
Grievous, General
  Invisible Hand **193**
  Malevolence **192**
  Soulless One **94**
GS-100 salvage ship **162**
Gungan battle wagon **67**
Gungan bongo submarine **79**
GX1 short hauler **133**

H
H-2 executive shuttle **132**
H-type Nubian yacht **122**
Hailfire droid **68**
Halo **148**
Hammerhead corvette **189**
Haor Chall Engineering 68, 125, 126, 128, 139, 174, 185
Hardcell-class interstellar transport **175**
HAVw A6 Juggernaut **71**
HMP (Heavy Missile Platform) droid gunship **16**
Home One **199**
Hound's Tooth **149**
Hover tank, Umbaran **52**

Huppla Pasa Tisc Shipwrights Collective 29, 92, 93, 127, 203
Hutt swamp speeder **78**
Hyena-class bomber **91**

I
IG-227 *Hailfire*-class droid tank **68**
IGV-55 surveillance vessel **164**
Imperial assault tank **72**
Imperial cargo ship **165**
Imperial construction module **203**
Imperial courier craft **144**
Imperial freighter **163**
Imperial Interdictor **186**
Imperial landing craft **143**
Imperial light carrier **187**
Imperial listener ship **164**
Imperial shuttle **142**
Imperial Star Destroyer **196**
Imperial troop transport **53**
Incom Corporation 14, 20, 100, 116
Interdictor cruiser **186**
Invisible Hand 12, **193**
ISP (Infantry Support Platform) speeder **41**
ITT (Imperial Troop Transport) **53**

J
J-type 327 Nubian starship **168**
J-type diplomatic barge **169**
J-type star skiff **123**
Jabba the Hutt, *Khetanna* **54**
Jedi ambassador shuttle **130**
Jedi speeder bike **32**
Jedi starfighters 96, **97**
Jedi turbo speeder **9**
Jendirian Valley **160**
Joben T-85 speeder **37**
Jumpspeeder **32**

K
Kamino submarine **80**
Kashyyyk, Battle of 16, 19, 57, 69, 71
Khetanna **54**
Kom'rk-class fighter **102**
Koro 2 airspeeder **8**
Krennic, Orson, *Delta*-class T-3c shuttle **141**
Kryze, Duchess Satine
  Coronet **195**
Kuat Drive Yards 61, 62, 63, 64, 65, 71, 80, 81, 165, 183, 196, 197

Kuat-Entralla Engineering 201, 202
Kuat Systems Engineering 97, 99, 112, 146, 152

L

LAAT (Low Altitude Assault Transport) 17
Lambda-class T-4a shuttle 142
Lancer-class pursuit craft 154
Landspeeders 39
Lantillian short hauler 133
Libertine 173
Lucrehulk-class cargo freighter 191
Luke's landspeeder 43
Luxury yacht 172

M

Malevolence 122, 192
MandalMotors 33, 42, 102, 103, 135, 154, 158
Mandalorian police speeder 42
Mandalorian shuttle 135
Mandalorian speeder 33
Mandalorian starfighter 103
Maul, Darth
  Scimitar 124
  speeder bike 28
Maxillipede shuttle 128
MC75 star cruiser 198
MC80A star cruiser 199
MC85 star cruiser 200
Meson Martinet 170
Millennium Falcon 21, 106, 156, 196
Mining Guild TIE fighter 111
Moogan gunship 151
MSP80 hover pod 18
MTT (Multi-Troop Transport) 46
Munificent-class star frigate 181

N

N-1 starfighter 77, 89
Naboo, Battle of 15, 40, 46, 67, 89, 161, 191
Naboo royal cruiser 169
Naboo royal starship 168
Naboo star skiff 123
Naboo starfighter 89
Naboo water speeder 77
Nantex-class territorial defense starfighter 92
Nebulon-B escort frigate 190
Neimoidian escort shuttle 125
Nightsister speeder 35
NR-N99 *Persuader*-class droid enforcer 69
Nu-class transport 129

O

Oevvaor jet catamaran 19
OG-9 homing spider droid 56
OMS (One Man Submersible)
  Devilfish Sub 81

P, Q

Pantoran cruiser 152
Pelta-class frigate 183
Perpetuus 170
Phantom 138
Phantom II 139
Phoenix Home (Imperial light carrier) 187
Phoenix Home (*Pelta*-class frigate) 183
Pirate tank 51
Pod hunter 87
Podracers
  Anakin's 26
  Sebulba's 27
Police speeders 13, 42, 44
Pongeeta-class speeder 78
Praxis Mk. 1 turbo speeder 9
Profundity 198
Providence-class dreadnought 193
Pteropter 18
Punworcca 116-class interstellar sloop 127
Quadjumper 159
Quarren UTS Pike 82
Quarrie 113, 114
Quasar Fire-class cruiser-carrier 187

R

Raddus 200
Rainhawk-class transport 152
Rebel airspeeder 20
Rebel gunship 115
Rebel transport 178
Redemption 190
Republic attack cruiser 194
Republic attack shuttle 129
Republic frigate 182
Republic medical frigate 183
Republic shuttle 170
Republic tugboat 158
Resistance bomber 121
Resistance starfighter 120
Resistance transport 180
Resurgent-class star destroyer 201
Rey's speeder 38
Rogue-class starfighters 104
Rothana Heavy Engineering 12, 17, 50, 58, 59, 72, 177
RZ-1 A-wing interceptor 112

S

Sail barge, Jabba's 54
Sandcrawler 73
Sato's Hammer 155
Scarif, Battle of 22, 23, 115, 157, 178, 188, 189, 198
Scimitar 124
Sebulba's podracer 27
Sentinel-class shuttle 143
Separatist supply ship 76
Shadow Caster 154
Sheathipede-class transport

shuttle 125
Phantom II 139
Sheathipede-class Type B cargo shuttle 126
Shekelesh-class freight gunship 151
Short-distance hyperdrive pod 88
Shuttle bus 11
Sienar Fleet Systems 22, 23, 105, 106, 107, 108, 109, 110, 111, 118, 141, 142, 143, 144, 186
Sienar-Jaemus Fleet Systems 119, 145, 179
Ski speeder 45
Skywaker, Anakin, podracer 26
Skywalker, Luke, landspeeder 43
Slave I 146
Slayn & Korpil 9, 98, 114, 121, 130, 132
Snowspeeder 20
Solar sailer 127
Solo, Han
  Eravana 167
  Millennium Falcon 156
SoroSuub Corporation 13, 39, 40, 43, 168, 172, 187
Soulless One 94
Spacetugs 158, 159
Separatist frigate 181
Special Forces TIE fighter 118
Speeder bus 11
SPHA-T (Self-Propelled Heavy Artillery Turbolaser) 58
Spider droid 56
SS-54 assault ship 148
STAP (Single Trooper Aerial Platform) 15
Star Commuter 2000 140
Star Destroyers
  Finalizer 201
  Imperial 196
  Republic attack cruiser 194
Starhawk speeder 34
Stealth ship 184
Stun tank 50
Subjugator-class heavy cruiser 192
Subpro Corporation 100, 159
Super tank 49
Supremacy 202
Swamp speeders 41, 78
Syndulla, Hera, *Ghost* 153

T

T-6 shuttle 130
T-16 Skyhopper 14
T-65 X-wing starfighter 116
T-70 X-wing starfighter 120
Tactical infiltration pod 88
Tantive IV 86, 188
Taylander shuttle 137
Techno Union starship 175
Theed Palace Space Vessel Engineering Corps 77, 89, 122, 123, 169

Theta-class T-2C shuttle 134
TIE Advanced v1 108
TIE Advanced x1 109
TIE bomber 106
TIE defender 110
TIE fighters 105
  Mining Guild 111
  Special Forces 118
TIE interceptor 107
TIE reaper 23
TIE silencer 119
TIE striker 22
Trade Federation battleship 191
Trade Federation landing ship 174
Tri-fighter 95
Tribubble bongo 79
Trident-class assault ship 83
TSMEU-6 personal wheel bike 70
Tugboat 158
Turtle Tanker 150
Twilight 147
TX-225 Occupier tank 72

U, V, W

U-wing gunship 115
Ubrikkian Industries 53, 54, 55, 78
Umbaran hover tank 52
Umbaran starfighter 101
Underground transport craft 154
Underwater Turbo Sled Pike (UTS) 82
Undicur-class jumpspeeder 32
Upsilon-class shuttle 145
V-19 Torrent starfighter 98
V-wing starfighter 99
Vader, Darth
  Executor 197
  TIE Advanced X1 109
VCX-series auxiliary starfighter 138
Venator-class Star Destroyer 99, 194
Vulture droid 90
Vulture-class starfighter 90
Vulture's Claw 162
Weequay pirate saucer 136
Wessell, Zam, Zam's airspeeder 8
wheel bike 70
WLO-5 speeder tank 51
Wookiee Catamaran 19

X, Y, Z

X-34 landspeeder 43
X-wing starfighters 100
  T-65 X-wing 116
  T-70 X-wing 120
Xanadu Blood 104
Y-wing starfighter 117
Yavin, Battle of 109, 116
YT-1300f light freighter 156
YT-2400 light freighter 155
V-666 light freighter 149
Zeta-class cargo shuttle 144
Zygerrian slave ship 161

ACKNOWLEDGMENTS

 Penguin Random House

Editors Matt Jones, Lauren Nesworthy
Senior Editor David Fentiman
Senior Designers Owen Bennett, Robert Perry
Project Art Editor Jon Hall
Designer Chris Gould
Senior Pre-Production Producer Jennifer Murray
Senior Producer Mary Slater
Managing Editor Sadie Smith
Managing Art Editor Vicky Short
Publisher Julie Ferris
Art Director Lisa Lanzarini
Publishing Director Simon Beecroft

Additional design by Amazing15
Edited by Simon Hugo

DK would like to thank Samantha Holland at Lucasfilm,
Marcus Scudamore and Martin Stiff at Amazing15, Helen Peters
for the index, Natalie Edwards and Alexander Evangeli for image
research, Hannah Gulliver-Jones, Shari Last, and Julia March
for editorial assistance.

For Lucasfilm
Senior Editor Brett Rector
Asset Management Newell Todd, Gabrielle Levenson, Bryce Pinkos,
Erik Sanchez, Tim Mapp, Nicole LaCoursiere, Shahana Alam
Art Director Troy Alders
Story Group Leland Chee, Pablo Hidalgo, Matt Martin

First American Edition, 2018
Published in the United States by DK Publishing
345 Hudson Street, New York, New York 10014

Page design copyright © 2018 Dorling Kindersley Limited
DK, a Division of Penguin Random House LLC
18 19 20 21 22 10 9 8 7 6 5 4 3 2 1
001–307148–Apr/2018

© & TM 2018 LUCASFILM LTD.

A catalog record for this book is available from the Library of Congress.
ISBN 978-1-4654-6665-5

DK books are available at special discounts when purchased in bulk for
sales promotions, premiums, fund-raising, or educational use. For details, contact:
DK Publishing Special Markets, 345 Hudson Street, New York,
New York 10014 SpecialSales@dk.com

Printed and bound in China

A WORLD OF IDEAS:
SEE ALL THERE IS TO KNOW

www.dk.com
www.starwars.com

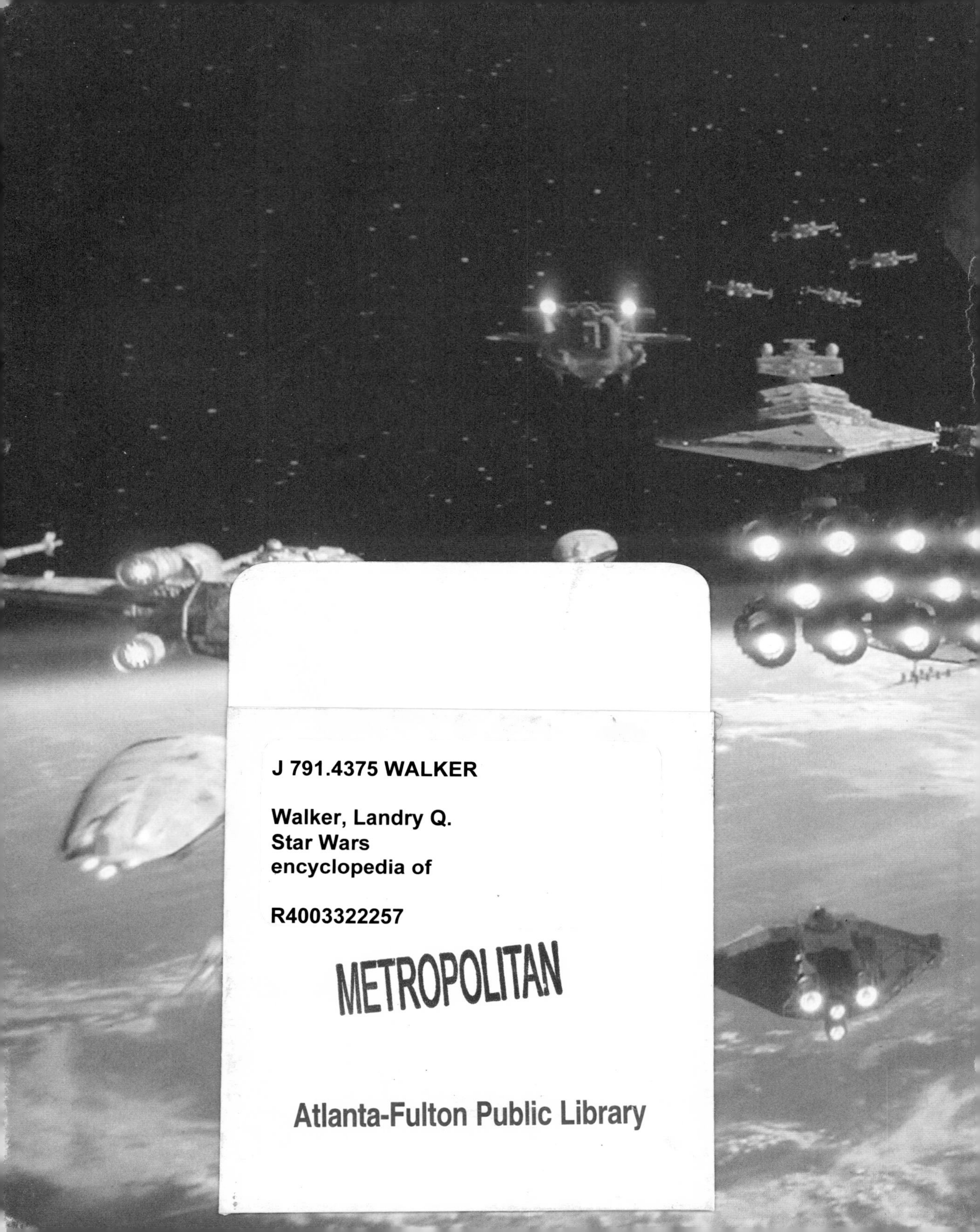